**New Directions for
Teaching and Learning**

Catherine M. Wehlburg
EDITOR-IN-CHIEF

Experiential Education:
Making the Most of Learning Outside the Classroom

Donna M. Qualters
EDITOR

Number 124 • Winter 2010
Jossey-Bass
San Francisco

EXPERIENTIAL EDUCATION: MAKING THE MOST OF LEARNING OUTSIDE
THE CLASSROOM
Donna M. Qualters (ed.)
New Directions for Teaching and Learning, no. 124
Catherine M. Wehlburg, Editor-in-Chief

Microfilm copies of issues and articles are available in 16mm and 35mm,
as well as microfiche in 105mm, through University Microfilms, Inc.,
300 North Zeeb Road, Ann Arbor, MI 48106-1346.

NEW DIRECTIONS FOR TEACHING AND LEARNING (ISSN 0271-0633, elec-
tronic ISSN 1536-0768) is part of The Jossey-Bass Higher and Adult
Education Series and is published quarterly by Wiley Subscription
Services, Inc., A Wiley Company, at Jossey-Bass, 989 Market Street, San
Francisco, CA 94103-1741. Periodicals postage paid at San Francisco,
CA, and at additional mailing offices. POSTMASTER: Send address
changes to New Directions for Teaching and Learning, Jossey-Bass, 989
Market Street, San Francisco, CA 94103-1741.

New Directions for Teaching and Learning is indexed in CIJE: Current
Index to Journals in Education (ERIC), Contents Pages in Education
(T&F), Current Abstracts (EBSCO), Educational Research Abstracts
Online (T&F), ERIC Database (Education Resources Information
Center), Higher Education Abstracts (Claremont Graduate University),
and SCOPUS (Elsevier).

SUBSCRIPTIONS cost $89 for individuals and $259 for institutions, agencies,
and libraries in the United States. Prices subject to change.

EDITORIAL CORRESPONDENCE should be sent to the editor-in-chief,
Catherine M. Wehlburg, c.wehlburg@tcu.edu.

www.josseybass.com

CONTENTS

FROM THE SERIES EDITOR

About This Publication

Since 1980, *New Directions for Teaching and Learning* (NDTL) has brought a unique blend of theory, research, and practice to leaders in postsecondary education. NDTL sourcebooks strive not only for solid substance but also for timeliness, compactness, and accessibility.

The series has four goals: to inform readers about current and future directions in teaching and learning in postsecondary education, to illuminate the context that shapes these new directions, to illustrate these new direction through examples from real settings, and to propose ways in which these new directions can be incorporated into still other settings.

This publication reflects the view that teaching deserves respect as a high form of scholarship. We believe that significant scholarship is conducted not only by researchers who report results of empirical investigations but also by practitioners who share disciplinary reflections about teaching. Contributors to NDTL approach questions of teaching and learning as seriously as they approach substantive questions in their own disciplines, and they deal not only with pedagogical issues but also with the intellectual and social context in which these issues arise. Authors deal on the one hand with theory and research and on the other with practice, and they translate from research and theory to practice and back again.

About This Volume

This volume is intended to help administrators, faculty, and staff in the creation of innovative and meaningful experiential education. Some of the most exceptional and transformative learning experiences happen outside of the classroom, so those in higher education should know how this type of engagement can benefit learning.

Catherine M. Wehlburg
Editor-in-Chief

CATHERINE M. WEHLBURG is the assistant provost for Institutional Effectiveness at Texas Christian University.

EDITOR'S NOTES

As the cost of education increases, endowments decline, and the job market tightens, institutions of higher learning are faced with many challenges: How do we remain relevant in a world that may still view us as the "ivory tower"? If we bring in the outside world, how do we convince our own faculty of the value of learning outside the classroom? How do we help students reflect deeply so as to acquire the knowledge and skills they will need in the future?

One of the most eye-opening moments for me as a professor was reading Richard Light's book *Making the Most of College: Students Speak Their Minds*, and realizing that some of the most powerful learning experiences students identified in college occurred outside the classroom. This fact was further brought home to me at a recent professional meeting; I was talking to a high school principal who begged me as an education faculty member to please "teach your students something useful" about being in a real classroom. His previous experience with teacher training programs showed they produced teachers who knew a lot about educational theory and very little about being a teacher.

This book grew out of my learning from a number of my own experiential experiences. First, as related above, it came from my need to understand how to make the most of in-the-field experiences for teacher candidates. Second, I learned from my experience as a faculty member at Northeastern University at a time when the institution was wrestling with defining cooperative education and fitting it into the pantheon of experiential education. Lastly, it came about because of wonderful summers spent with the Martha's Vineyard Experiential Institution, sponsored by Northeastern University and the World Association of Cooperative Education. Here was the "think tank" of experts from around the country (and later the world) struggling together to define experiential education and outline best practices for incorporating it into the education of the future generation. As Tim Donovan, one of the founders of the Institute, put it:

> We wanted to fully understand this enterprise for which Northeastern had become so well known but also to broaden the focus to include study abroad, service-learning, undergraduate research, and related forms. Through MVI, we taught ourselves what we had already been doing at Northeastern for some time, as well as how we might do it more effectively in the future. We

were also encouraged enough to think in terms of others we might "teach" as part of a project that would be national and even international in scope.

The chapter authors of this volume are all experienced, passionate experiential educators who fervently believe in the value of learning from experience and who are daily bringing it into their own practice as teachers and administrators.

This volume contains an overview of the forms and issues in experiential education. It goes on to discuss in detail how to operationalize these different forms. These chapters will help you design, construct, reflect, assess, fund, and engage colleagues in understanding the power of experiential education.

Besides our authors, I owe a debt of gratitude to Tim Donovan, Jim Stellar, and Rick Porter, founders and visionaries of the Martha's Vineyard Institute. Lastly, this book could not have come about without the work of Alana Lenhart, undergraduate experiential researcher extraordinaire! Alana took on this adventure with me as an undergraduate researcher and as in all good experiential education activities, I learned as much from her as she did from me. She is a talented student, precise editor, and the best assistant any editor could ask for.

As you read through this volume, the authors hope that you will consider how you can enrich your students' learning through experience and judge for yourself the power of experiential experiences.

Donna M. Qualters
Editor

Reference

Light, R. J. *Making the Most of College: Students Speak Their Minds.* Cambridge, MA: Harvard University Press, 2001. (ED 462 042)

DONNA M. QUALTERS is the director of the Center for Teaching Excellence and an associate professor of education and human services at Suffolk University in Boston, Massachusetts.

NEW DIRECTIONS FOR TEACHING AND LEARNING • DOI: 10.1002/tl

1

This chapter introduces some of the forms and practices of experiential education and raises some challenging questions about the role that pedagogy plays in institutions of higher learning.

Forms and Issues in Experiential Learning

David Thornton Moore

Programs falling under the general rubric of *experiential education* take a number of forms, varying on several dimensions; what is offered here is a schematic overview. In general, they all involve students in activities that look rather different from more traditional classroom-based methods: the formal lecture and discussion, the reading assignment, and the sit-down examination. Although these experiential activities go by different names in different program formats, they share the core characteristic of students' direct engagement in productive work outside the classroom. In some way, the activity is thought to bring the student-intern in contact with the phenomena, concepts, and problems addressed in classes, curricula, and disciplines (Sweitzer and King, 2004).

Experiential Learning Approaches and Forms

The various approaches to experiential learning share some philosophical and theoretical foundations, as well. Nearly everyone cites John Dewey, from *How We Think* (1910) to *Experience and Education* (1938), drawing out the simple principle that "experience is the best teacher." More subtly, they use Dewey's conception of learning as an active process of grappling with conditions and problems in the world; constructing and testing solutions; and interacting with others to make sense and make progress. Some of them acknowledge with Dewey (1938) that not all experience is educative, that some experience can thwart or discourage further learning.

Many draw on David A. Kolb's *Experiential Learning* (1984) as a theory about how learners apprehend and transform various kinds of knowledge

NEW DIRECTIONS FOR TEACHING AND LEARNING, no. 124, Winter 2010 © Wiley Periodicals, Inc.
Published online in Wiley Online Library (wileyonlinelibrary.com) • DOI: 10.1002/tl.415

based in experience; in certain circles, this text is a bible for practitioners. Others cite Donald A. Schön's *The Reflective Practitioner* (1983) for its discussion of how professionals think in action. Still others have advocated the use of theories of situated cognition (Kirschner and Whitson, 1997), activity (Engeström, Miettinen, and Punamaki, 1999) and practice (Chaiklin and Lave, 1993) as a way of understanding learning as a function of experience (see Moore, 1999a). Most often, though, advocates of experiential learning focus more on practical matters than on theory.

Those practices vary on several key dimensions: their programmatic forms and activities, their missions and philosophies, their constituencies and participants, their pedagogical practices, their locations in the university or college, and their claims about impacts and results. What follows constitutes a brief review of some of those forms.

Internships. Considered the most generic of the terms used to denote experience-based learning activities by college students, the word *internship* is sometimes used by people in both service-learning programs and cooperative education for the out-of-classroom element of their students' work; people in the liberal arts disciplines such as sociology and psychology also use it to refer to the field component of their courses. Even those noncredit programs based in career services offices use the word.

In structure, the internship may be a free-standing activity not connected to a classroom, the experiential equivalent of an independent study: A student gets credit (the amount depends on hours per week spent in the field) for working in a business, a social agency, or a cultural or governmental institution. She may work alongside regular employees of the organization, or may execute a specialized project on her own or in a small team; she may sit in on staff or board meetings or attend public events; she may interview or observe certain people to get a sense of what goes on there. Conversely, the internship may be an add-on to a classroom course, an activity conceptually related to the theme and substance of the class, in which the student spends, say, three or four hours a week volunteering in a social agency or shadowing a corporate executive. On the other hand, the internship may *not* be for school credit, but still entail direct work in some kind of organizational setting.

Internship programs typically articulate several kinds of missions: exploring the intersection between theory and practice (Sweitzer and King, 2004, p. 9), career exploration and development (Fedorko, 2006), or personal and professional development (Inkster and Ross, 1995). They also make various claims about enhancing critical thinking and conceptual understanding, responsible and ethical behavior, and the capacity to work with diverse people. Some are contained in an academic unit; others are found in an interdepartmental space under the provost; and still others are housed in career services or community service offices.

Pedagogical practices vary across forms and schools, as well. Most credit-bearing programs require some form of guided reflection: learning contracts, journals, written papers, and sometimes concurrent seminars (Sweitzer and King, 2004; Milnes, 2003). In Chapter 5 of this volume, Joseph A. Raelin more fully explores this work-based form of experiential education.

Service-Learning. Perhaps the most widely analyzed form of experiential learning in higher education is service-learning: out-of-classroom community service activity combined with the study of academic concepts and theories. The precise relationship between those two major elements is a matter of some controversy. Some practitioners focus on the service; others stress thinking through theory (Stanton, Giles, and Cruz, 1999). Most, however, do insist on at least some degree of reflection on the experience, on exercises, discussions, and readings that place the service work in historical, sociological, and political contexts (Eyler and Giles, 1999; Butin, 2005).

The missions of service-learning programs focus on the twin dimensions of enhancing student learning and development and meeting social needs and promoting social change (Butin, 2005). Practitioners of service-learning tend to rest their work explicitly on ethical and political principles: for example, social justice or celebration of diversity (Stanton, Giles, and Cruz, 1999).

Service-learning activities are often attached to courses as either required or optional components, especially in departments in the social sciences and professions. A student in a course on urban poverty, for instance, might be required to spend three hours a week in a homeless shelter or soup kitchen; students in an international relations course in a New York City college might work an afternoon a week in a U.N. agency or in a nongovernmental organization (NGO). To varying degrees, the course instructors might draw on students' internship experiences as part of their discussions of issues such as economic development or human rights.

A number of texts offer pedagogical suggestions for service-learning practitioners (Schoenfeld, 2004; Cress, Collier, Reitenauer, and Associates, 2005). More systematic research has been done in the realm of service-learning than in any other form of experiential education. A peer-reviewed quarterly, the *Michigan Journal of Community Service Learning*, publishes studies ranging from evaluations of student impacts to theoretical explorations of ethics. A decade ago, Janet Eyler and Dwight E. Giles (1999) offered a book cleverly titled *Where's the Learning in Service-Learning?*, arguing among other things that learning from service depends on serious and extensive reflection. More recently, Dan W. Butin (2005) edited an anthology on "critical issues and directions" in service-learning at the university level.

Cooperative Education. The third major form of experiential learning began in 1906 at the University of Cincinnati as a way of combining the school-based transmission of technical expertise with the traditional benefits of first-hand experience in the mechanical trades (Ryder, 1987, pp.

3–5). The core function of co-op education centers on building students' career skills and knowledge (Howard, 2004, p. 3). Although a few co-op programs operate in liberal arts colleges (Linn, Howard, and Miller, 2004), most serve preprofessional students in fields such as engineering, business, and healthcare.

The pedagogical strategies underlying co-op programs vary, but virtually all entail periods of work coordinated with periods of study. The conceptual connections between the direct experience and the classroom study are explored to varying degrees through varying pedagogies. Some institutions, especially those using a parallel format, insist on explicit and extensive reflection on the experience back at school; others appear to assume that the transfer from classroom to workplace is obvious, a matter of "application" (Ryder, 1987). Research on cooperative education is fairly extensive and tends to focus on questions of student effects (retention, performance in the major, career choice, starting salaries, post-graduation employment performance, and similar parameters) and on issues of institutionalization (administering and funding programs, attracting faculty support, and so on). *The Journal of Cooperative Education* is an excellent resource for learning more about this model of experiential education.

Other Models. While internships, service-learning, and cooperative education represent the most widespread forms of experiential learning, several others are common. One may be called student-faculty research, or undergraduate research experience (URE): the use of undergraduates as research assistants and collaborators by faculty members engaged in their own investigations (Kardash, 2000).

Community-based research (CBR), discussed by Elise Dallimore, David A. Rochefort, and Kristen Simonelli in Chapter 2, is a growing form of experiential learning in which faculty and students cooperate with local organizations to conduct studies that somehow meet the needs of communities. While CBR might be regarded as a form of service-learning, it can also be seen as a social science version of the laboratory, in which students gain firsthand experience of the process of formulating and pursuing researchable questions (Strand, Marullo, Cutforth, Stoeker, and Donohue, 2003).

Study abroad can be regarded in some ways as a form of experiential learning, as Lori Gardinier and Dawn Colquitt-Anderson argue in Chapter 3. Students not only take courses in regular classrooms, they also participate in a wide variety of culturally challenging encounters simply by living in a new place; moreover, some study abroad programs encourage students to do internships and service-learning with local businesses, nonprofits, and cultural organizations.

Issues in Experiential Education

Advocates of experience-based learning in higher education make a passionate case for the benefits of this program and pedagogy (Kaye, 2004).

Some evidence does suggest that, at least under certain conditions, it enhances student learning and development (Eyler and Giles, 1999; Linn and others, 2004; see various issues of the *Michigan Journal for Community Service Learning*, the *Journal of Cooperative Education*, and the *NSEE Quarterly*). Moreover, a number of commentators, particularly in service-learning, have addressed important issues related to experiential learning in higher education (Jacoby and Associates, 1996; Butin, 2005). In the remainder of this chapter, however, I want to identify and explore two major challenges that I believe face the field: whether experience is an appropriate source of learning in higher education, and, if it is, whether existing pedagogical methods realize its potential. I will take a position on these issues, but only tentatively.

The Mission Question. The first problem is whether experience *belongs* in the university, whether the fundamental purposes of higher education are served by students' working in businesses, government agencies, and arts institutions, or providing service in community-based organizations. The answer depends, of course, on one's conception of the mission of higher education—and on that score, there is deep division. There are *idealists* who see the university as a place for the study of classic texts, pure science, and theories unencumbered by practical realities (Bloom, 1987; Hart, 2001). Even Stanley Fish (2001), certainly no cultural conservative, argues that the university should only teach students to understand and produce scholarship. Fish has no problem with internships and community service—so long as they do not count toward graduation or earn grades (p. 21). On the other hand, *pragmatists* argue that the university should serve practical social purposes, though with a deep commitment to democratic values. Clark Kerr (1963/2001) is the leading example; Adrianna J. Kezar and her colleagues (2005) are more recent voices for that stance.

Another way to frame the question focuses on the forms of knowledge propagated by traditional university instruction and by direct work experience: Are they compatible? Bent Flyvbjerg (2001) provides a tool for addressing that issue by drawing on Aristotle's distinction among three kinds of intellectual virtue: (1) *episteme*, often translated as "science," is certain knowledge of the objective, the eternal, the universal, the rational (p. 55–56); (2) *techne*, sometimes called "art" or "craft," is "an activity [that is] concrete, variable and context-dependent" and whose "objective is application of technical knowledge and skills according to a pragmatic instrumental rationality" (p. 56); and (3) *phronesis*, translated as "prudence" or "practical common sense," goes beyond objective or instrumental knowledge to reach *judgment*, the process of deliberating not just on what *is*, but on what is *good* in relation to values and interests embedded in the context.

At the risk of oversimplifying, I will argue that the modes of knowing most common in the university tend toward *episteme* and *techne*. Especially in the liberal arts, and particularly in the "hard" sciences, students learn about universals, about decontextualized concepts and theories. Even in the humanities, analysis is expected to be rational, a systematic interaction between the knower and the text. Knowledge in the epistemic sense is not about *application*, about the concrete; it is about the general, the abstract.

Professional education could be regarded as *teche*-based, but in most professional schools, faculty in fact seek a merger between *episteme* and *techne*: They focus on activity that is "context-dependent," but they attempt to impose regularities—theories, best practices—on that activity; they provide students with rough-and-ready rules and frameworks designed to tell them what to do in concrete practice.

The university is *not*, however, prone to engaging in phronetic inquiry, according to Flyvbjerg (2001). Faculty tend to pose questions like "how can I best understand this phenomenon?" (whether the phenomenon is the behavior of subatomic particles or the meaning of a Greek tragedy), or "what works on this problem?" (whether the problem is treating a child with autism or planning a new town).

Activity in the "real world" tends to engage participants more often in *phronesis*. There is always an element of improvisation, of bricolage, of seat-of-the-pants problem-solving, based in concrete situations but requiring judgments about the good and the right and the effective. Of course there are "best practices" manuals that try to smooth out contextual variations; and of course ethical deliberations are sometimes less than rigorous. But situated activity inevitably goes beyond the epistemic and the technical.

There is a second useful framework for analyzing the relation between knowledge-use in school and in the sites where students do internships and community service: theories of situated cognition and situated learning. The basic argument of this school of thought is that people think and learn differently in different social contexts (Kirschner and Whitson, 1997; Lave and Wenger, 1999): they formulate problems differently; they use different logics to solve those problems; they apply different criteria to judging ideas and actions. Jerome Bruner (1996) describes different "frames for thinking," or ways of making meaning—the actional, the propositional, the interpretive, the normative—and argues that different social contexts tend to favor one mode over the other. Clearly, the university tends to privilege the propositional-scientific, whereas real-world behavior tends toward the actional mode.

If we accept the premises of the situated cognition theorists, and return to the mission question, we can refine the problem: If experiential learning varies significantly from academic learning in terms of the nature of knowledge-use generally practiced in the university, does it really belong there? Clearly, there is a problem of fit: the kinds of knowledge-use in the workplace or service site do not map easily onto the kinds of knowledge propounded by the college curriculum.

That lack of fit does not settle the mission question. One could argue that the function of higher education *should* be revised to include enhancing students' capacity to engage in phronetic, actional, ethical, and contextualized forms of knowledge-use in a variety of situations. William M. Sullivan and Matthew S. Rosin (2008) lay out a new mission for higher education focused on bridging the existing chasm between theory and practice, between objective science and normative action. Thomas R. Bailey, Katherine A. Hughes, and David Thornton Moore (2004) conclude that, under certain circumstances and given certain practices, experience can be a meaningful and productive element of school-based learning.

Still, there is great resistance to experience-based programs among many faculty, administrators, and theorists of higher education. Many academics object to what they perceive as a political bias among practitioners of experiential learning (Bloom, 1987). They see progressive politics driving these programs, and question whether that leaning disqualifies them as an academic enterprise. Others, like Fish (2001), simply think experience is not an appropriate source of scholarly knowledge.

The Pedagogy Question. Let us assume, for the sake of argument, that a strong case can be made for incorporating experience into the curriculum and pedagogy of the university, that experience is a legitimate source of higher learning. The second question I propose to address is whether our teaching strategies make good educational use of that opportunity. Coming at the issue from another direction, what value is added by the university to the inherent educational value of the direct experience of work or service? I am asking this question on a conceptual level; I do not propose to review the literature on student outcomes in experience-based programs, but only to raise some concerns about pedagogy.

Imagine this case: A student is taking a course on organizational sociology, where she is reading Max Weber on bureaucracy; during the same term, she is doing an internship with the New York City Department of Education, one of the world's great bureaucracies. My question is this: What educational benefit does she get by doing those two things at the same time? Does she use Weber to understand the dynamics of her experience at the office? Does her experience at the office enrich her grasp of Weber? What might her professor do to enhance the synergy between these two modes of knowledge?

Part of the problem stems from the insight about situated cognition: What are the terms by which this student would explore the intersection between Weber and her work? At the internship site, she thinks in an actional mode: How can I bring these people together for a meeting? If I bring up this issue to my boss, will she think I'm stupid? Weber, on the other hand, operates at the level of organizational patterns—systems of rules, career paths, modes of leadership—not at the level of personal experience. So how does one form of thinking enhance the other? I once interviewed a student who was doing an internship at a municipal planning agency as part of a course on urban politics; I asked him if any of his readings connected to his experience, and he mentioned Marx: "It's all about power, right?" That "application" of Marx to the contingencies of his agency's work seems fairly thin.

One way theorists discuss this problem is by raising the question of *transfer of learning*: How and under what conditions does knowledge from one context carry over into another? David N. Perkins and Gavriel Salomon (1989) found that transfer does occur, but only when someone calls the learner's attention to the connections and encourages her to examine them repeatedly. Similarly, Janet Eyler and Dwight E. Giles, Jr. (1999) found that the impact of service-learning on such cognitive skills as understanding the complexities of a social problem depends on the intensity of the reflection process: the effects do not show up with even moderate reflection. A number of practitioner-theorists have insisted on the crucial importance of reflection as an element of experiential pedagogy (Weil and McGill, 1989; Boud, Cohen, and Walker, 1993). These pedagogical strategies do exist, and they can be effective *if* they are pursued rigorously.

But there are factors constraining the efficacy of school-based practices for enhancing experiential learning. For one thing, students often resist it: They tend to care more about doing the work than about reflecting on it; and they often see the internship as a mode of career exploration, as a foot in the door, and not primarily as a learning experience. My own observation in the course of interviewing college interns and observing service-learning courses is that the instructor sometimes has to pull teeth for students to do the rigorous reflection. Or they do it, but on a personalistic and emotional level: "My boss is such a jerk!" or "I really felt like an adult!" These conversations are useful entries into deeper and larger issues and ideas—but it takes some persistence to get them to go there.

Without interrogating the work or service experience with some degree of intensity, the student gains little from its straddling the academic and the real worlds. The value added by the school, I would argue, is minimal in that case: The student could have learned the same things just by virtue of having a part-time job or service activity. Experiential pedagogy, done right, is extremely rewarding—but also extremely demanding (Moore, 1999b).

Concluding Remarks

A very large portion of college students these days do internships, cooperative education, or service-learning. The common wisdom among college students today is that an internship is a crucial element of their higher education experience, especially as a strategy for easing the transition to a career. Indeed, the proportion of students who do internships of one kind or another at some point during their undergraduate careers may be exceeded only by the number of them who post to their Facebook pages.

The typical student, that is, spends some time in an organized, recognized, sometimes accredited out-of-classroom but school-sponsored learning activity: working in a business or a medical center; performing some kind of community service; participating in an Alternative Spring Break project; engaging in field-based research to fulfill the requirements of a course.

If these experiences are structured effectively and processed rigorously, they can add a great deal of value to students' learning and to the educational strength of the university. In fact, they have the potential to transform higher education, to broaden and deepen the nature of knowledge and learning that goes on in the college, and to alter the relationship between student and teacher and between university and community.

But these transformative effects depend on careful planning and execution, on avoiding the tendency to fall back on the adage that "every experience is educational," on pushing students—and faculty—to think rigorously and extensively about the intersections between theory and practice. We need to foster critical thinking through decisive methods of instruction, so students can understand not only how to do things, but why they work the way they do, and what ethical principles are at stake as they engage in real-world activity.

References

Bailey, T. R., Hughes, K. L., and Moore, D. T. *Working Knowledge: Work-Based Learning and Education Reform*. New York: RoutledgeFalmer, 2004.

Bloom, A. *The Closing of the American Mind: How Higher Education Has Failed Democracy and Impoverished the Souls of Today's Students*. New York: Simon and Schuster (Touchstone), 1987.

Boud, D., Cohen, R., and Walker, D. (eds.). *Using Experience for Learning*. Bristol, PA: Open University Press, 1993. (ED 371 169)

Bruner, J. "Frames for Thinking: Ways of Making Meaning." In D. R. Olson and N. Torrance (eds.), *Modes of Thought: Explorations in Culture and Cognition*. New York: Cambridge University Press, 1996.

Butin, D. W. (ed.). *Service-Learning in Higher Education: Critical Issues and Directions*. New York: Palgrave Macmillan, 2005.

Chaiklin, S., and Lave, J. (eds.). *Understanding Practice: Perspectives on Activity and Context*. New York: Cambridge University Press, 1993.

Cress, C. M., Collier, P. J., Reitenauer, V. L., and Associates. *Learning through Serving: A Student Guidebook for Service-Learning across the Disciplines*. Sterling, VA: Stylus, 2005.

Dewey, J. *How We Think*. Mineola, N.Y.: Dover, 1997 (originally published 1910).

Dewey, J. *Experience and Education*. New York: Collier, 1938.

Engeström, Y., Miettinen, R., and Punamaki, R-L. (eds.). *Perspectives on Activity Theory*. New York: Cambridge University Press, 1999.

Eyler, J. and Giles, D. E., Jr. *Where's the Learning in Service-Learning?* San Francisco: Jossey-Bass, 1999.

Fedorko, J. *The Intern Files: How to Get, Keep, and Make the Most of Your Internship*. New York: Simon Spotlight, 2006.

Fish, S. *No Angel in the Classroom: Teaching through Feminist Discourse*. Lanham, MD: Rowman and Littlefield, 2001.

Flyvbjerg, B. *Making Social Science Matter*. New York: Cambridge University Press, 2001.

Hart, J. *Smiling through the Cultural Catastrophe: Toward the Revival of Higher Education*. New Haven: Yale University Press, 2001.

Howard, A. "Cooperative Education and Internships at the Threshold of the Twenty-first Century." In P. L. Linn, A. Howard, and E. Miller (eds.), *Handbook for Research in Cooperative Education and Internships*. Mahwah, N.J.: Lawrence Erlbaum Associates, 2004.

Inkster, R. P., and Ross, R. G. *The Internship as Partnership: A Handbook for Campus-based Coordinators and Advisors*. Raleigh, NC: National Society for Experiential Education, 1995.

Jacoby, B., and Associates. *Service-Learning in Higher Education: Concepts and Practices*. San Francisco: Jossey-Bass, 1996.

Kardash, C. M. "Evaluation of an Undergraduate Research Experience: Perceptions of Undergraduate Interns and Their Faculty Mentors." *Journal of Educational Psychology*, 2000, 92(1), 191–201.

Kaye, C. B. *The Complete Guide to Service Learning: Proven, Practical Ways to Engage Students in Civic Responsibility, Academic Curriculum, & Social Action*. Minneapolis, MN: Free Spirit Publishing, 2004.

Kerr, C. *The Uses of the University*. Cambridge, MA: Harvard University Press, 2001 (originally published 1963).

Kezar, A. J., Chambers, T. C., and Burkhardt, J. C. *Higher Education for the Public Good: Emerging Voices from a National Movement*. San Francisco: Jossey-Bass, 2005.

Kirschner, D., and Whitson, J. A. *Situated Cognition: Social, Semiotic, and Psychological Perspectives*. Mahwah, NJ: Lawrence Erlbaum Associates, 1997.

Kolb, D. A. *Experiential Learning: Experience as the Source of Learning and Development*. Englewood Cliffs, NJ: Prentice-Hall. 1984.

Lave, J., and Wenger, E. *Situated Learning: Legitimate Peripheral Participation*. New York: Cambridge University Press, 1991.

Linn, P. L., Howard, A., and Miller, E. (eds.). *The Handbook for Research in Cooperative Education and Internships*. Mahwah, NJ: Lawrence Erlbaum Associates, 2004.

Milnes, J. *Field Work Savvy: A Handbook for Students in Internship, Co-operative Education, Service-learning and Other Forms of Experiential Education*. Enumclaw, WA: Winepress Publishing, 2003.

Moore, D. T. "Toward a Theory of Work-based Learning." *IEE Briefs* 23, 1–6, 1999a.

Moore, D. T. "Behind the Wizard's Curtain: A Challenge to the True Believer." *NSEE Quarterly*, January–February, 1999b.

Perkins, D., and Salomon, G. "Are Cognitive Skills Context-bound?" *Educational Researcher*. 1989, 18(1), 16–25.

Ryder, K. G. "Social and Educational Roots." In K. G. Ryder and J. W. Wilson (eds.), *Cooperative Education in a New Era: Understanding and Strengthening the Links between College and the Workplace*. San Francisco: Jossey-Bass, 1987.

Schoenfeld, R. M. *Service-Learning—Guide and Journal*. Higher Education Edition. Seattle, WA: Guide and Journal Publications, 2004.

Schön, D. A. *The Reflective Practitioner: How Professionals Think in Action*. New York: Basic Books, 1983.

Stanton, T. K., Giles, D. E., Jr., and Cruz, N. *Service-Learning: A Movement's Pioneers Reflect on its Origins, Practice, and Future*. San Francisco: Jossey-Bass, 1999.

Strand, K., Marullo, S., Cutforth, N., Stoecker, R., and Donohue, P. *Community-Based Research and Higher Education: Principles and Practices*. San Francisco: Jossey-Bass, 2003.

Sullivan, W. M., and Rosin, M. S. *A New Agenda for Higher Education: Shaping a Life of the Mind for Practice*. San Francisco: Jossey-Bass, 2008.

Sweitzer, H. F., and King, M. A. *The Successful Internship: Transformation and Empowerment in Experiential Learning.* Belmont, CA: Brooks/Cole-Thomson, 2004.

Weil, S. W., and McGill, I. (eds.). *Making Sense of Experiential Learning: Diversity in Theory and Practice.* Bristol, PA: SRHE and Open University Press, 1989.

DAVID THORNTON MOORE *is an associate professor and the director of the Community Learning Initiative in the Gallatin School of Individualized Study at NYU.*

2

Community-based learning and research is one of the most exciting ventures in contemporary higher education. This chapter examines programs and practices focusing on administrative structure as well as three specific classroom-based models.

Community-Based Learning and Research

Elise Dallimore, David A. Rochefort, Kristen Simonelli

The origins of community-based learning and research (CBLR) are found in a variety of precursor activities, including the "action research model" first promoted by Kurt Lewin in the 1940s and the more recent practices of "participatory research" associated with development planning in the third-world (Strand, Marullo, Cutforth, Stoecker, and Donohue, 2003; Stoecker, 2002). As more voices call for higher education to engage the world beyond the campus walls (Benson, Harkavy, and Puckett, 2007), CBLR continues to offer an excellent means for fulfilling this responsibility.

A University Model

Community-based learning and research can be integrated with many types of experiential education. Whatever the context, CBLR focuses on engaging faculty, community-based organizations, and students in partnerships to actively meet academic-learning and community goals (Cress, Collier, Reitenauer, and Associates, 2005). At Northeastern University, cooperative education, student research, global experience, and service-learning (S-L) are the focus of the institution's commitment to "experiential learning." CBLR is taking place in all these different forms and contexts. As such, S-L is the primary academic context in which CBLR involves students in fulfilling the experiential mission, doing so through mutually-beneficial partnerships between faculty-led academic courses and community-based nonprofit organizations. These experiences, which combine service and learning in both classroom and community settings, allow students to

NEW DIRECTIONS FOR TEACHING AND LEARNING, no. 124, Winter 2010 © Wiley Periodicals, Inc.
Published online in Wiley Online Library (wileyonlinelibrary.com) • DOI: 10.1002/tl.416

develop an understanding of course-specific knowledge and skills and apply them, as well as disciplinary/professional norms, while gaining a sense of civic responsibility. Other distinctive components of S-L include the implementation of reflection and evaluation/assessment, thus helping ensure both community and academic needs are being met (Bringle and Hatcher, 1995).

The S-L process begins with the S-L coordinator recruiting faculty members. In some cases, the faculty member already has a relationship with a nonprofit organization or approaches the S-L coordinator for assistance in accessing the program resources and network. To identify appropriate matches, a "Request for Partnerships" (RFP) is conducted. Faculty and community partners are provided a packet of resources that assist in conceptualizing how to integrate course and service roles/projects, including specific language used within our S-L program since language may differ even within a university.

Although universities may conceptualize and implement CBLR somewhat differently, best practices ring true across institutions (Honnet and Poulson, 1989), and valuable resources can be found in journals or books published on this topic (for example, the *Michigan Journal of Community Service Learning*) and government-sponsored programs through the Corporation for National and Community Service. Additionally, assessment tools such as Andy Furco's (2002) "Self-Assessment Rubric for the Institutionalization of Service-Learning in Higher Education" can be used to determine how well S-L is accepted within the institutional curriculum and culture.

At Northeastern, S-L resides within the university's Center of Community Service reporting to the Office of Government Relations and Community Affairs. This strategic reporting structure enhances awareness of political, social, and economic issues affecting our local community, individual community-based nonprofit organizations, and community groups. While working collaboratively with campus and community partners, the S-L program works to ensure constituents understand how CBLR complements their existing objectives (meeting the needs of boards, clients, funders), engaging students within "our" community, preparing them as professionals, and integrating community experiences back into experiences on campus.

To structure the program to grow and address the interests of each key constituent, Northeastern's program has four focal areas:

1. *Strategic Campus and Community Partnerships*, which involve nurturing relationships with S-L advisory board and faculty members, community-based nonprofits, the Office of the Provost, and national and state offices that support civic engagement to stay current on various interests.
2. *Technical Support and Resources*, focusing on course, partnership, and professional development and sustainability.

NEW DIRECTIONS FOR TEACHING AND LEARNING • DOI: 10.1002/tl

3. *Student Development and Leadership*, offering courses utilizing S-L in multiple disciplines and across academic levels so that students may engage with our community throughout their academic careers. We offer tours of our four primary communities to complement organization-based orientations and broaden student appreciation for the assets and challenges of the communities which they serve. The S-L teaching assistant program also provides opportunities for students to support the partnerships and integration of service and learning goals, and assist with projects such as faculty recruitment or resource development.

4. *Promotion, Assessment, Evaluation, and Recognition* to promote pedagogy to balance research demands that often take priority over teaching and service responsibilities. Promotion includes center and S-L program specific newsletters, brochures, and Web sites. The S-L program facilitates online evaluation tools for all members of the partnership. These tools work to assess the program resources, course-specific learning objectives, each partnership, and whether students meet learning and service goals. Finally, although events to recognize the contributions of all parties are often difficult to schedule, they can be important reminders of broader campus and community goals.

CBLR in Practice

We turn now to three specific curricular examples of CBLR. While placing different emphases on service and research, they nonetheless share the values of community engagement, learning-by-doing, and guided reflection, all hallmarks of CBLR.

Direct Service-Learning Model. Referred to by Heffernan (2001) as Discipline-Based Service-Learning, students taking introductory to mid-level courses fulfill learning objectives by providing direct service in a community-based nonprofit. This occurs on a weekly basis while they engage in ongoing guided reflection of their experiences using course content as a basis for their analysis and understanding.

"Interpersonal Communication" utilizes an S-L model where students serve directly with one of several community-based nonprofit organizations. Service sites are selected through a process that first matches needs identified by local community partners with the course curriculum. Further, students are offered a choice regarding the populations they serve and the type of services provided. For example, student options range from teaching English for Speakers of Other Languages (ESOL) to immigrant adults to providing tutoring and mentoring for students in an after-school program. Students fulfill a minimum of two hours per week, with the emphasis on fulfilling a semester-long commitment to a community partner.

Process and Examples. The true integration of service and learning goals begins immediately when students submit a "Community Partner Selection" form and attend required training and orientation. The course is structured so students engage in ongoing reflection about their service and think critically about how their experiences provide new insights about interaction with others (accomplished through home-learning assignments, in-class discussion, research assignments, and application papers). Further, they discuss and analyze their experiences with classmates sharing placements and then provide an analysis of their collective experience in the form of a group presentation.

Outcomes. The outcomes of this project are best captured through student and client perspectives:

"No other text book or lecture could force me to apply course concepts to my communication (course) as much as service-learning has been able to. Not only am I participating in a service activity . . . , but it has been useful in helping me grasp abstract concepts . . . ."

"Her [Elise Dallimore's] ability to push students beyond the university setting and into the broader community . . . supports her commitment to . . . academic excellence, real work experience, and urban engagement. . . ."

Project-Based Service-Learning Model. Referred to by Heffernan (2001) as Problem-Based Service-Learning, students taking mid- to advanced-level undergraduate- or graduate-level courses serve (in teams) with the community partner, "much as 'consultants' working for a 'client'" (pp. 2–7). Within this model, staff in the administrative units of an organization, provide students with projects that they do not have the time or resources to address. Students in more advanced courses should come with specific knowledge and skills that they can pair with current course material to make recommendations or develop solutions to the challenges identified by the community partner.

The "Consultation Skills" course utilizes the project-based model to assess organizational needs, conduct benchmarking data, and then provide recommendations for organizational change. The partnership is maintained over years, so students build on the work done by previous classes. This assignment is designed to give students first-hand experience to: (1) utilize the instructional frameworks which guide the course, and (2) apply the consulting techniques and strategies they have read about, discussed, and utilized in case examples.

Process and Examples. The course is structured so that students engage in consulting activities as part of an ongoing consulting project. While this involves a number of interim deliverables (see Exhibit 2.1), the project culminates with a client presentation and written project report in which consulting groups outline the consulting services, the data that were collected and analyzed, the conclusions drawn, and recommendations for change.

Exhibit 2.1. Service-Learning Consultation Project

Consultation Skills Assignment

Rationale and Project Description

It is important for prospective consultants to be able to assess organizational problems and create appropriate recommendations for change. This service-learning project is designed to facilitate engagement in consulting activities.

In completing this assignment, students will:

1. Apply consulting techniques and strategies from the text and class discussions to a real consulting situation
2. Use the instructional frameworks which serve as the basis for the course
3. Use a research model to assess one organization and its employees
4. Engage in data collection, analysis, and interpretation in order to address issues of organizational functioning and communication
5. Provide justification for the actions recommended to the organizations drawn from readings from this and other courses, as well as additional research
6. Present an assessment of diversity issues or concerns and recommendations—including concrete goals, strategies for implementation, and assessment tools—to address such issues in both an oral presentation and a written summary

Project Deliverables

For this assignment, students must:

1. Individually review and evaluate the organizational data to determine which materials relate to issues of diversity and therefore will be relevant to analysis
2. Attend an onsite orientation
3. Conduct organizational and benchmarking research including relevant diversity-related goals in use by benchmarked organizations and statistics on Boston-area nonprofits, individuals living in Boston, and individuals living in the state of Massachusetts

Diversity Benchmarking Research Draft Due

4. Complete data analysis and interpretation stages to understand the diversity concerns
5. Prepare a force field analysis of the organization

Draft of S-L Data Analysis and External Research

6. Prepare and deliver a 15–20 minute presentation of your work

Consultation Presentation for Client

7. Produce one 15-page summary of your analysis, including: (a) an analysis of the organization, using *each phase* of the research model, (b) a summary of benchmarking statistics, and (c) a well-developed list of diversity goals, implementation strategies, and assessment tools reflecting the data analysis process and, thereby, utilizing organizational data, course materials, and outside research to justify recommendations for change

Final Client Consultation Report Due

Outcomes. A student comment includes:

"[This] class . . . allows me to consult for a nonprofit organization, and develop some of the complex skills associated with management consulting . . . . I feel stimulated by the challenges that it presents."

A client comment includes:

"The students . . . data analysis formed the basis of findings that we reported directly to all staff, management and our Board of Directors. We simply could not have accomplished this very successful project without the students' assistance . . . ."

Community-Based Research. The community-based research (CBR) or community-based action research model refers to "a partnership of students, faculty, and community members who collaboratively engage in research with the purpose of effecting social change" (Strand, Marullo, Cutforth, Stoecker, and Donohue, 2003, p. 3). CBR represents "a way of working" that stresses community involvement in the design and execution of studies, adapts methods of data collection to the demands of the topic, and often draws on quantitative and qualitative approaches simultaneously (Green and others, 1997).

Northeastern University's Community-Based Research Initiative (CBRI), established in 2002, won 2007 grant funding from the National Community-Based Research Networking Initiative of Learn and Serve America/The Corporation for National and Community Service. Reflecting the specialization of its director, CBRI focuses on issues of public policy, drawing on research strategies and topics of interest from within this field.

Northeastern's CBRI possesses a threefold purpose. First, students learn about the substance of new policy issues, they assist in the practical application of research techniques, and they develop professional skills through such activities as community consultation, public speaking, data analysis, and report preparation. Second, CBRI contributes to the university's outreach commitment. Third, CBRI influences the realm of public affairs by helping to inform community members and other stakeholders about policy issues, filling in gaps in data, and advocating for positive social change.

Process and Examples. Seven CBRI projects have been completed. The range of policy topics has been extensive, from media treatment of mental health issues to state laws on recycling and more. Every project was the fruit of collaboration with a community partner, most frequently a public interest advocacy group (Massachusetts Public Interest Research Group, for one example).

Northeastern's CBRI follows a comprehensive course-based approach in that each project serves as the sole focus of a semester-long practicum.

Enrolled students function as a research team contributing to an overall project via individual and group assignments. The faculty member acts as the team leader or research director. A single overriding goal guides the work of the team: to complete the final report that has been promised to the community partner. Project selection occurs in idiosyncratic ways, the result of outreach by the project director or requests from community groups and agencies. Project implementation begins with a getting-acquainted stage during which the community partner and research team meet, the instructor and students inventory skills within the group, and background research on the topic is conducted. A longer second phase of eight to ten weeks is devoted to the bulk of project research. Depending on methodology, this phase may consist of interviews, surveys, examination of documents, and other data collection. As analysis is completed, students also begin to draft sections of the report. The third phase is the hectic closing period when the report must be finalized. The team then presents its findings, together with concrete recommendations for organizational, administrative, and legislative changes, to the community partner. For maximum project impact, the community partnership must continue beyond the practicum by disseminating project results to all target audiences—community members, organized stakeholder groups, public officials—with interest in, or responsibility for, the policy issue.

Outcomes. Outcome measurement for CBR must reflect its multidimensional goals. Student participants have praised the practicum for its "relevance to [my] professional and academic aspirations," "the opportunity to understand the various pitfalls and frustrations that can be a part of the research process," and "the chance to do real research and contribute to a study that could impact policy."

Through CBRI, community partners acquire capacity for data collection and analysis at no cost to them. Consider the following message of appreciation received from one local library director following distribution of the report on budgetary cuts for public library services in Massachusetts:

"I want to share this remarkable study ["Massachusetts Public Libraries at Risk"] not only with my trustees, but also with my selectmen, finance committee, and legislators!"

CBRI's ultimate purpose is to impact politics and society. Quick or easy change is not a likely possibility for the major controversies we have studied. However, the modest role played by these projects in expanding awareness and understanding issues on the local public policy agenda offers encouraging evidence of CBRI's effective engagement with the world beyond academia.

Conclusion

Community-Based Learning and Research provides opportunities for institutions of higher education to achieve their goals of educating students, advancing teaching and scholarship, and meeting real needs of under-resourced communities and nonprofit organizations. By providing successful examples of campus and community partnership, this chapter has aimed to demonstrate how CBRL can enhance individual learning experiences and the culture and curriculum of an institution, while making a lasting social impact.

References

Benson, L., Harkavy, I., and Puckett, J. *Dewey's Dream: Universities and Democracies in an Age of Education Reform.* Philadelphia: Temple University Press, 2007.

Cress, C. M., Collier, P. J., Reitenauer, V. L., and Associates. *Learning through Serving: A Student Guidebook for Service-Learning across the Disciplines.* Sterling, VA: Stylus, 2005.

Furco, A. *Self-Assessment Rubric for the Institutionalization of Service-Learning in Higher Education.* University of California, Berkeley, 1999. Based on the Kacskes/Muyllaert Continuums of Service Benchmark Worksheet. Revised 2002.

Green, L.W., George, M.A., Daniel, M., Frankish, C.J., Herbert, C.P., Bowie, W.R., and O'Neil, M. (1997). Background on Participatory Research. In D. Murphy, M. Scammell, and R. Sclove, eds., *Doing Community-Based Research: A Reader.* Amherst, MA and Knoxville, TN: The Loka Center in partnership with Community Partnership Center, pp. 53–66.

Heffernan, K. "Fundamentals of Service-Learning Course Construction." *RI: Campus Compact,* 2001, 2–7, 9.

Honnet, E. P., and Poulson, S. J. *Principles of Good Practice for Combining Service and Learning.* (Wingspread Special Report). Racine, WI: The Johnson Foundation, 1989.

Stoecker, R. "Practices and Challenges of Community-Based Research." *The Journal of Public Affairs.* Supplemental Issue 1: Civic Education and Higher Education, 2002, *VI,* 219–239.

Strand, K., Marullo, S., Cutforth, N., Stoecker, R., and Donohue, P. *Community-Based Research and Higher Education: Principles and Practices,* San Francisco: Jossey-Bass, 2003.

ELISE DALLIMORE is an associate professor in the Department of Communication Studies with a joint appointment in the College of Business Administration at Northeastern University.

DAVID A. ROCHEFORT is an Arts and Sciences Distinguished Professor of political science at Northeastern University.

KRISTEN SIMONELLI is the associate director and service-learning coordinator in the Center of Community Service at Northeastern University.

NEW DIRECTIONS FOR TEACHING AND LEARNING • DOI: 10.1002/tl

3

This chapter outlines the range of program models for studying abroad and provides readers with specific structural- and curricula-based approaches for internationalizing campuses.

Learning Abroad

Lori Gardinier, Dawn Colquitt-Anderson

Institutions are increasingly interested in internationalizing campuses. According to the International Association of Universities, seventy-three percent of members believe that internationalization of their campuses is "very much" a priority at their institution (Knight, 2003). This chapter will provide models that use both structural and curricular methods to internationalize campuses, highlighting practical issues such as student selection and legal considerations.

NAFSA: Association of International Educators identifies four program models used for developing education abroad (Brockingtong, Hoffa, and Martin, 2005). The first is *integrated*, in which participants enroll in foreign universities as visiting, nonmatriculated students. Students are selected by the foreign universities and must satisfy prerequisites for selected courses. The second model is *unintegrated*, which gives the sending institution more control over the curriculum, duration, faculty selection, and experience because students are taking university-sponsored courses abroad. It is usually topic-specific, has limited course options, and is sponsored by a particular academic department. It is an option for students who are not ready for more independence and deeper cultural immersion or students in underrepresented majors with rigid curriculum outlines. The third model, growing in popularity for its flexibility to accommodate an increasingly diverse student population, is the *hybrid*. This model allows universities to respond quickly to a field reliant upon foreign systems. It offers more immersion than unintegrated programs and more support than integrated programs. The fourth model, *independent*, is a highly individualistic model

New Directions for Teaching and Learning, no. 124, Winter 2010 © Wiley Periodicals, Inc.
Published online in Wiley Online Library (wileyonlinelibrary.com) • DOI: 10.1002/tl.417

23

that is ideal for students who will conduct research with faculty support abroad while experiencing the deepest level of immersion. Once students meet the preapproved requirements, the university issues the academic credit.

Identifying and Addressing Risks and Liability

Global instability requires universities to review emergency response plans. Each term, directors must be prepared for expected emergencies involving lost or stolen property, illnesses, and so on. Occasionally, serious incidents will occur. Recent events involving natural and manmade disasters, civil unrest, and global health concerns have prompted more institutions to act by purchasing software, such as Terra Dotta, that allows them to instantly track and communicate with students and faculty abroad and access emergency contact information.

Students need information on exercising appropriate caution and making sound judgments from predeparture to reentry, so they can get the most out of this experience while respecting the culture and preparing for the unexpected. Orientations, usually mandatory, can help students adjust while informing them of the risks specific to their locations. Most institutions require travel insurance as a condition of participation. Institutions in the United States are charged with meeting diverse student needs and adhering to mandates of the Americans with Disabilities Act; however, the same standards do not apply in many foreign locations. For this reason, programs must incorporate measures to ensure students apply where adequate support is available. Mobility International USA (2010) provides additional resources on disabilities and studying abroad.

Liability waiver forms prepared by university counsel are a must. Sometimes, parental signatures are required, especially for locations for which the U.S. State Department has issued a Travel Warning. Travel Warnings and Alerts are available on the State Department (2010) Web site. A useful strategy for education abroad administrators is to create accessible location-specific scenarios for students, promoting a uniform message. Lastly, faculty leading programs abroad must fully understand the university's established emergency protocol and have access to this information while abroad (see Rhodes, 2005).

Considering Underrepresented Groups

The Institute of International Education's 2008 *Open Doors* survey confirms that over the past decade the dominant group of study abroad participants is white female social science majors. Johnnetta B. Cole (1990) identifies "The Five F's" as barriers to study abroad: family, faculty, finances, fear, and friends. These obstacles can be placed into three categories: institutional, financial, and cultural.

NEW DIRECTIONS FOR TEACHING AND LEARNING • DOI: 10.1002/tl

A rigid curriculum is often an *institutional barrier*. To remove this barrier, align program and campus policies as much as possible and involve relevant offices in the process. Furthermore, identify a study abroad contact in each major office who can serve as a study abroad specialist and communicate needs and changes to them. An example of a *cultural barrier* is when a student lacks role models or experience traveling beyond their community and is fearful of unfamiliar environments. To remove this barrier, education abroad office staff should reach out personally to potential students to discuss ways of working study abroad into their academic plans and work closely with campus representatives. Being available to speak to parents, who can be very influential in students' decisions, is also important. A *financial barrier* is one that is most familiar, because many students need financial assistance and the search to find it can be overwhelming. The Institute of International Education's funding source directory, *IIE Passport* (2010), can be a great resource. It serves as a clearinghouse for programs that provide financial assistance for all students. The education abroad office can also collaborate with the financial aid office to reach out to TRIO and Pell Grant recipients and encourage those students to apply for the Gilman, NSEP Boren, and Fulbright scholarships.

Curricular Methods: Globalizing Institutions through Faculty-Led Programs

Internationalizing college campuses can occur through structural means or through enhancing the academic curricula. This section will focus on how faculty can internationalize their content through short-term faculty-led abroad experiences. Currently, short-term programs are serving the largest number of American students studying abroad, including community college students and others whose financial or academic needs prohibit a longer stay (Institute of International Education, 2008). In addition to the high percentage of students participating in short-term programs, an American Council on Education Report (Green, Luu, and Burris, 2008) found that institutions are increasing support for faculty who lead study abroad programs.

The increase in short-term study abroad models has generated research on the impact of such programs on students, providing some preliminary evidence that short-term programs can have a positive impact in areas such as students' intercultural sensitivity (Lawton and others, 2006). Tammy L. Lewis and Richard A. Niesenbaum (2005) found a range of benefits for students who participated in their short-term international program, including an increase in student willingness to take courses outside of their major, increased confidence to travel abroad in longer-term programs, increased interest in interdisciplinary studies, and a more sophisticated perception of the costs and benefits of globalization. Research has shown that leading international programs also have a positive impact on globalizing and enriching an instructor's domestic teaching (Sandgren and others, 1999).

NEW DIRECTIONS FOR TEACHING AND LEARNING • DOI: 10.1002/tl

Faculty-led programs can provide a combination of the following: discipline-specific cultural comparison of practice or theory, foreign language instruction, exchange with students from local universities, and an opportunity to attend lectures by local academics or practitioners from the host country; some include a service-learning component. Generally, the cost to the student is also less than traditional semester-long programs, making study abroad accessible to a broader student population. Faculty-led programs are also great for building support among faculty, for expanding international research collaborations, and as feeders into longer full-semester programs or internships.

Structure, Roles, and Relationships. Several key factors promote successful short-term faculty-led programs, including academic rigor, use of mixed teaching methods, and facilitated reflection synthesizing experiences with academic content. There is no formula for the percentage of time that should be spent in formal class time, seeing cultural/historical sites and events, doing field work, or engaging in peer-to-peer cultural exchange. Regardless of the mix, students should arrive at the destination with a grounding in both the academic and cultural context through a combination of predeparture lectures, guided research, online discussions, readings, and cultural events relevant to the trip.

Faculty leaders have an expanded and complex role in leading such programs, and require institutional support to succeed in leading short-term programs. This altered role involves administrative and leadership skills not typically used in the classroom.

Students will see the faculty member in a range of settings from humbling to humiliating, and the delicate lines of authority from the classroom cannot be sustained. Conversely, faculty may see students in compromising situations. Appropriate conduct within faculty-student relationships is rarely discussed; generally, the discourse is limited to sexual harassment. However, with the multiplicity of roles that the faculty leader assumes in these programs, appropriate boundaries become critical. There is not full agreement on what constitutes appropriate faculty-student behaviors within relationships. Maryka Biaggio, Tana Lucic Paget, and M. Sue Chenoweth (1997) provide a framework for faculty when considering the ethics of dual relationships with students, and it is useful when faculty negotiate the more complicated dimensions of leading a short-term program abroad.

- *Acknowledging Power and Responsibility of Faculty Role.* Although it can be easy to slip into a more egalitarian dynamic as you are coexperiencing life abroad, it is important for faculty to remember that dual relationships can be confusing and potentially harmful to students.
- *Developing a Frame for Evaluating Faculty-Student Relationships.* Provide yourself with some specific parameters for how, when, and where you will relate to students during the program. One of the most meaningful

aspects of these programs is for the students to have the opportunity to relate with faculty in a more holistic way. However, it is important to have clear guidelines on the extent to which you are involved in the assignments and projects, as your increased presence and involvement can blur these lines as well.

• *Fostering a Climate for Ethical Relationships.* Running a program abroad can be very demanding on faculty physically, emotionally, and psychologically. Faculty needs to ensure that their needs are met without inappropriately impinging on relationships with students (Owen and Zwahr-Castro, 2007).

One of the most challenging aspects of this programming is violation of campus codes, most especially alcohol policies. Depending on the location, students may have greater access to alcohol than they do in the United States, which can promote a level of consumption that is disproportionally high. Faculty should check with their home institution on policies surrounding alcohol use. It is understood that the student code of conduct is applicable in settings abroad, particularly when they are participating in a university-sponsored program. Faculty should utilize the expertise of on-campus leaders in counseling and education roles to develop strategies for responding to troubling alcohol use.

Service-Learning in Short-Term Faculty-Led Programs. Faculty using service-learning internationally have the opportunity to offer similar learning benefits to students in international settings, further enriching the cultural exchange. Sara Grusky (2000, p. 859) defines international service-learning as "an organized excursion taken by students (and often faculty or administrators) to different countries or different cultures where students and faculty live with local families and immerse themselves in a culture that is distinct from their own. Students work with local organizations to serve the community where they are staying, engage in a cultural exchange, and learn about a daily reality very different from their own." Initial studies reveal high levels of student satisfaction with their international service learning experiences (Gaines-Hanks and Grayman, 2009; Knutson Miller, Kim-Han, and Gonzalez, 2006).

Faculty should consider the unique skills and resources inherent in their discipline that could have benefits for local organizations. Problem-solving/project-based models are a good way to structure international service-learning because they are intended to be shorter term, have a specific goal and time frame, utilize the particular strengths of a group, and have the potential for a tangible benefit to the partner organization or community.

Students who apply to these programs are often motivated to work for social or economic change, but need to be realistic about their potential for impact. Ultimately, the greatest beneficiary in the international service-learning relationship is often the student. A student's participation in these programs has the potential for learning that reverberates throughout their academic and professional career while providing an opportunity to promote personal development.

Students embarking on international service-learning also need to consider the ethical dimensions of engaging in community-based work abroad. I will often require students to read Ivan lllich's 1968 speech, "To Hell with Good Intentions," renouncing international volunteerism, and then to articulate some of the main critical points. Using this as a starting point, I will facilitate a dialogue on how they might be perceived in the host community and the mixed attitudes on international volunteerism they may experience.

Faculty must also promote models that maintain high ethical standards. A useful predeparture activity is to have students apply service-learning scenarios specific to your location against your discipline's code of ethics. Andrea Chapdelaine, Ana Ruiz, Judy Warchal, and Carole Wells (2005) have developed a code of ethics for service-learning that may be a useful resource for these types of classroom activities.

Conclusion

This chapter provided readers with emerging and established structural and academic models for internationalizing institutions of higher education. The range of study abroad models can be applied to meet an institution's unique goals for providing students with meaningful international experiences. Faculty-led program are exciting models that have the potential to transform both students and leaders. As they continue to expand, we can expect innovative models that combine both structural and academic dimensions to emerge that build on lessons learned in other forms of experiential education.

References

Biaggio, M., Paget, T. L., and Chenoweth, M. S. "A Model for Ethical Management of Faculty-Student Dual Relationships." *Professional Psychology: Research and Practice,* 1997, 28(2), 184–189.

Brockingtong, J. L., Hoffa, W. M., and Martin, P. *NAFSA's Guide to Education Abroad for Advisers and Administrators,* 3rd ed. Washington, DC: NAFSA: National Association for International Educators, 2005.

Chapdelaine, A., Ruiz, A., Warchal, J., and Wells, C. *Service-Learning Code of Ethics.* Bolton: Anker Publishing Company, 2005.

Cole, J. B. "Opening Address of the 43rd International Conference on Educational Exchange." In Council on International Educational Exchange (ed.), *CIEE: Council on International Educational Exchange Annual Conference International Education: Black Students and Overseas Programs: Broadening the Base of Participation.* Charleston, S.C.: Council on International Educational Exchange, 1990, 1–8. (ED 340 323)

Gaines-Hanks, N., and Grayman, N. "International Service-Learning in South Africa and Personal Change: An Exploratory Content Analysis." *NASPA Journal, 46*(1), Art. 5,

2009. Retrieved October 22, 2009, from http://publications.naspa.org/naspajournal/vol46/iss1/art5

Green, M. F., Luu, D., and Burris, B. "Mapping Internationalization on U.S. Campuses: 2008 Edition." Washington, D.C.: American Council on Education, 2008.

Grusky, S. "International Service Learning: A Critical Guide from an Impassioned Advocate." *American Behavioral Scientist*, 2000, *43*, 858–867.

Illich, Ivan. "To Hell with Good Intentions." Conference on InterAmerican Student Projects (CIASP) in Cuernavaca, Mexico, 1968. Retrieved November 1, 2009, from www.swaraj.org/illich_hell.htm.

Institute of International Education. "2008: Americans Studying Abroad." *Open Doors*. Institute of International Education, 2008. Retrieved March 12, 2010, from http://opendoors.iienetwork.org/?p=131592.

Institute of International Education. *IIE Passport: Study Abroad Directories*. Institute of International Education and Education Dynamics, 2010. Retrieved March 12, 2010, from www.iiepassport.org.

Knight, J. "Internationalization of Higher Education. Practices and Priorities: 2003 IAU Survey Report." International Association of Universities, 2003.

Knutson Miller, K., Kim-Han, J., and Gonzalez, A. M. "Outcomes Associated with Experiential Learning in Domestic and International Settings: The Voices of Preservice and Experienced Teachers." Paper presented at the annual meeting of the American Association of Colleges for Teacher Education, Jan. 6, 2006. Retrieved March 25, 2009, from www.allacademic.com/meta/p36191_index.html.

Lawton, P., Leigh, L., Rexeisen, R., and Hubbard, A. "Short-Term Study Abroad and Intercultural Sensitivity: A Pilot Study." *Journal of Intercultural Relations*, 2006, *30*(4), 457–469.

Lewis, T., and Niesenbaum, R. A. "The Benefits of Short-Term Study Abroad." *The Chronicle Review*, 2005, *51*(39), B20.

Mobility International USA. *Mobility International USA—MIUSA*. 2010. Retrieved March 12, 2010, from www.miusa.org.

Owen, P., and Zwahr-Castro, J. "Boundary Issues in Academia: Student Perceptions of Faculty—Student Boundary Crossings." *Ethics and Behavior*, 2007, *17*(2), 117–129.

Paige, M. R., Fry, G. W., LaBrack, B., Stallman, E. M., Josic, J., and Jon, J. "Oregon Study Abroad for Global Engagement: Results That Inform Research and Policy Agendas." Forum on Education Abroad Conference. Portland, OR, February 19, 2009.

Rhodes, G. "Crisis and Risk Management." *SAFETI Resources for Program Administrators*. The Center for Global Education: Safety Abroad First Educational Travel Information Clearinghouse (SAFETI), 2005. Retrieved March 12, 2010, from www.globaled.us/irl/crisis&risk.html.

Sandgren, D., Elig, N., Hovde, P., Krejci, M., and Rice, M. "How International Experience Affects Teaching: Understanding the Impact of Faculty Study Abroad." *Journal of Studies in International Education*, 1999, *3*(1), 33–56.

U.S. State Department. Bureau of Consular Affairs. "Current Travel Warnings." 2010. Retrieved March 12, 2010, from http://travel.state.gov/travel/cis_pa_tw/tw/tw_1764.html.

LORI GARDINIER *is the program director for human service at Northeastern University in Boston, Massachusetts.*

DAWN COLQUITT-ANDERSON *is the former director of the Office of International Study Programs at Northeastern University.*

NEW DIRECTIONS FOR TEACHING AND LEARNING • DOI: 10.1002/tl

4

"Operational and value-focused skills" and active learning strategies together with experiential opportunities found in performing arts programs bring integrity and quality to intentional learning and undergraduate liberal arts education in the twenty-first century.

Demystifying Experiential Learning in the Performing Arts

Nancy Kindelan

The pedagogy of performing arts courses in theatre, film, music, and dance programs found in most liberal arts curricula is clearly experiential insofar as the making of art involves active engagement in classroom activities or events that are staged or filmed. But because many educators outside the arts perceive performing arts programs as solely providing a platform for students to showcase their talents, they believe that the goals and objectives of performing arts curricula focus on developing technical skills over what educators call "operational" and "value-focused" skills (Doherty, Chenevert, Miller, Roth, and Truchan, 1997, pp. 170–176). This view fails to recognize that performing arts courses and projects include cognitively challenging endeavors that help to advance the intellectual skills necessary for managing lifelong career goals and for contributing to the social well-being of our nation. Therefore, the curricula of many performing arts programs support interdisciplinary and independent research projects, encourage reflective pedagogies of civic engagement, include service-learning activities and study abroad programs, and offer distinctive experiential ways of learning.

Well-planned experiential activities help performing arts students develop the critical thinking and leadership skills necessary in building and sustaining successful professional careers; navigate career choices throughout their lives; and become contributing members of society engaged in thinking about complex social issues and taking responsible civic action.

NEW DIRECTIONS FOR TEACHING AND LEARNING, no. 124, Winter 2010 © Wiley Periodicals, Inc.
Published online in Wiley Online Library (wileyonlinelibrary.com) • DOI: 10.1002/tl.418

31

When performance courses and projects do more than develop technical skills, they engage students in active learning experiences that address many of the goals and skills of a contemporary liberal education, especially those that strive to develop a twenty-first century workforce that is socially responsible.

Intersection of Liberal Education and Experiential Learning

Before going further, here are some fundamental thoughts about a liberal arts education in the twenty-first century. Current literature on the topic defines a liberal—or liberating—education as one that preserves the best traditions of the baccalaureate degree while at the same time meeting the public's demand for practical education.

The Association of American Colleges and Universities' landmark project, *Greater Expectations: A New Vision for Learning as a Nation Goes to College* (2002), and their more recent publication *College Learning for the New Global Century* (2007) promote a lasting education that assists undergraduates in meeting the challenges found in a contemporary world. Significantly, both reports support learning that is intentional; to that end, they encourage the development of learning strategies that help students become "empowered, informed, and responsible" members of society through activities that integrate, adapt, and apply classroom theories to real-world problems. Intentional learners are comfortable "in the context of a diverse world," value "difference and commonality," and act "in ethical and responsible ways" when facing contemporary situations (Association of American Colleges and Universities, 2002, pp. 21–28, 33). These documents note that the pedagogical practices of engagement (learning by doing)—in addition to the collaborative activities, integrative learning opportunities, and practical experiential strategies often found in performing arts projects—play a role in developing a deeper awareness of social problems.

The notion that undergraduate performing arts programs go beyond the realm of extracurricular entertainment and can speak to the aims of a contemporary liberal education is surprising to many educators and individuals outside the academy. Yet the curricula of challenging performing arts programs include: (1) the practice of gathering, analyzing, and synthesizing knowledge through collaborative team projects that culminate in a staged or filmed production; (2) research and written projects that rely on conceptual and reflective thought that results in cultural scholarship (a script or dramaturgical program); and (3) experiences that encourage intentional learning through participation in experiential activities such as service-learning projects, study abroad programs, or unique cooperative opportunities. These curricular and cooperative experiences are examples of how active learning strategies *and* experiential learning situations help students recognize that project-driven intentional learning activities are empowering and can lead to responsible social action.

Let me begin by casting a wider net, suggesting how learning strategies found in courses in performing arts departments, in combination with off-campus experiential opportunities in the field, help students develop the skills relevant to their undergraduate education and are transferable to work outside the profession. Integrative experiential opportunities help students develop the intellectual muscle to navigate complex social ideas and situations. I offer the following two points for clarity: (1) students who perform in a dance, play, or film are involved in the creative process of translating or adapting the author's story to the stage or film, and (2) scripts are viewed as a microcosm of the author's perception of significant social issues or cultural events within the context of a particular time and place. Thus, in the performance classroom/laboratory space and through active collaborative creation of a performance piece, students develop the ability to transfer this knowledge to the performance space through creating characters and theatrical images that illuminate something hidden or revelatory about how the script's environment affects the characters' struggle, and exchange thoughts with others about the social ideas embedded in the author's work. Because the creative process involves translating the script's ideas to the stage or film through the presentation of artful images, training in the performing arts involves active dramaturgical pedagogies that help students achieve these goals.

Additionally, performing artists are charged with the fundamental task of presenting clear, often evocative *and* provocative, interpretations of a story or composition. The creative process provides excellent examples of why performing arts departments seek ways to develop, through active pedagogies of engagement, "operational skills (communication and literacy, quantitative literacy, reasoning, interpersonal effectiveness)" and "value-focused skills (aesthetic responsiveness, citizenship, responsible participation in the global environment, ethics)" (Doherty, Chenevert, Miller, Roth, and Truchan, 1997, pp. 174–176).

Communication and literacy skills are desirable for all students who are interested in the performing arts. The development of these skills helps students who perform to organize, sharpen, and challenge their original perceptions. A significant part of performing arts curricula involves writing reflective journals that include observations about a character's struggle when facing a moral dilemma. Mathematical agility or *quantitative literacy* is a desirable skill when interpreting or writing a musical score or choreographing a dance. When artists address how social issues affect the psychology of characters, they apply *critical reasoning skills* of *integrative thinking and problem solving*. Creating art is about the integration of knowledge; therefore, wise performing arts students who seek a deeper understanding about a character's psychology and the play's social history will gather and synthesize information from other liberal arts courses when analyzing a character in preparation for performance. Finally, collaborative activities that involve *teamwork, interaction*, and *cooperative learning* are some examples illustrating *interpersonal effectiveness* skills. Performing artists tend to work in groups; they rely on each other's abilities to solve production problems as they strive to bring the performance to fruition.

Value-Focused Skill Development

But how do performing arts programs help students become artist/citizens or productive members of society? I believe part of the answer relies on the effective development of value-focused skills. In *College: The Undergraduate Experience in America* (1987), Ernest L. Boyer expresses his disapproval of higher education's tendency to emphasize specialized skills at the expense of developing the values of social awareness. He offers: "the values professionals bring to their work are every bit as crucial as the particularities of the work itself" (Boyer, 1987, pp. 110–111). Performing arts programs interested in presenting challenging projects to their students—projects that focus on the struggle for human rights, social justice, cultural equality, or environmental issues—have listened to Boyer and not allowed technical proficiency to overshadow the importance of value-focused skills.

This skill set includes "aesthetic responsiveness" (*interpreting works of art with an enlightened eye*), "citizenship" (*becoming socially engaged in the community*), "responsible participation in the global environment" (*being sensitive to multiple, cultural, and cross-cultural perspectives*), and "ethics" (*identifying complex dilemmas*) (Doherty, Chenevert, Miller, Roth, and Truchan, 1997, pp. 174–176). These skill sets are particularly beneficial to performing artists who create characters from other cultures and, therefore, must be comfortable crossing boundaries to ponder similarities and differences and recognize that the process of understanding social problems begins by giving the text an informed reading. Both value-focused skills and operational skills help performing arts students not only achieve a deeper understanding of their field and life, but also are transferable to other professions as well.

Challenge of Off-Campus Experiences

The challenge for performing arts programs is to discover ways to integrate learning and practice so that the active pedagogic experiences in the classroom and performance labs are enhanced through participation in off-campus experiential programs such as field experiences, internships, service-learning projects, study abroad programs, and cooperative job opportunities.

Quite clearly, cooperative programs that involve first-hand connections with the day-to-day operations of professional theaters help students determine whether or not they are interested in pursuing a career in this field. It is my opinion that experiential programs that occur outside the traditional classroom are most beneficial after undergraduates complete the

NEW DIRECTIONS FOR TEACHING AND LEARNING • DOI: 10.1002/tl

first two to three years of their baccalaureate degree. Consider how, at this point of their academic career, students might not be ready to perform professionally; however, they have accomplished a significant number of courses, read various plays that represent multiple perspectives and cultures, and participated in numerous laboratory performance projects. At this strategic moment of the student's academic career, traveling to another country is a more valuable experience because there is a stronger appreciation for cross-cultural and multicultural viewpoints. An internship in a professional opera company, regional theatre, or dance troupe is more meaningful because it is not so much about meeting the stars of the organization as it is about observing how the actors, directors, scenic designers and technicians make effective artistic choices that illuminate the social ideas in the play.

Case Study: The Laramie Project

The following example illustrates how the preparation of a theater student's undergraduate honors thesis on dramaturgy and *The Laramie Project* (a play by Moisés Kaufman and the Tectonic Theatre Company) promotes intentional learning through emphasizing critical thinking and analytical skills as well as developing leadership and citizenship skills. The production of *The Laramie Project* is an example of how theatre departments enhance the understanding of multiculturalism and social responsibility on the college campus through active and experiential learning strategies. *The Laramie Project* presents the story of Matthew Shepard, a homosexual student at the University of Wyoming, who in 1998 was found beaten and left to die, bound to a fence on the outskirts of town. The play unfolds through a series of encounters with townspeople from Laramie, Wyoming; the script is the result of a series of interviews conducted and arranged by the play's authors Moisés Kaufman and his Tectonic Theatre Company. In the fall semester of 2003, *The Laramie Project* was performed at Northeastern University under my directorship, with the collaboration of a student dramaturg.

The foundational basis of my student's capstone project on dramaturgy and social responsibility began in an earlier script analysis class in which she completed a four-week casebook study on *The Laramie Project*. Later, under my mentorship, we scheduled weekly meetings in the course of the next year, and the pedagogical practices of script analysis continued as we worked in partnership mining the world of Kaufman's play script. However, because she was now a member of an actual, not hypothetical, production team, she became responsible for identifying pertinent social questions and compiling specific interdisciplinary research relevant to the director's vision of the play. She moved beyond the hypothetical research experiences found in a curricular script analysis course and faced the authentic problems of a dramaturg working with an artistic team on an actual production of *The Laramie Project*.

NEW DIRECTIONS FOR TEACHING AND LEARNING • DOI: 10.1002/tl

In regional theatres, a professional dramaturg compiles research on a play in casebooks for the production team so that they can consider information about the play's social, cultural, historical, and literary history. Therefore, my student dramaturg assembled the results of her comprehensive research into casebooks that were distributed to each cast member. Her intent was to provide the actors with background information and data about the play—specifically the evolution of its historical events, material relevant to issues of social injustice, details about the environs of Laramie, Wyoming, and biographical notes about the actual people who told the story.

An additional responsibility of a dramaturg working in a regional theatre is the preparation of a dramaturgical program (a collection of articles, chronologies, pictures, interviews, and so on). Thus, my student compiled a twenty-page dramaturgical program intended to assist the university audience in gaining access to the play's literary background and social history.

The work of a professional dramaturg often involves outreach educational programs with high schools or opportunities for audiences to engage in conversations with the artistic team. My student was aware of these practices and outlined a community-service diversity project for high school students that focused on helping them face the play's complex social issues: hate crimes, homosexuality, and injustice. She planned a series of pre- and post-performance small-group sessions in which she and the students discussed the play's events and whether or not they felt the production helped them to unravel the social complexities within the Matthew Shepard story. To help her students analyze the play's ideas and production's images, she prepared a study guide for teachers that contained background information about Laramie and articles about the play.

Through active participation in advanced dramaturgical activities, in concert with a service-learning project and the completion of a reflective honors thesis, this student succeeded in accomplishing the best sense of intentional learning. She connected the classroom to the real life of a dramaturg and, in turn, recognized and wrote a thesis about how performance activities when focusing on issues of social responsibility are central not only to Northeastern University's cooperative mission, but also to the goals and objectives of higher education.

References

Association of American Colleges and Universities. *Greater Expectations: A New Vision for Learning as a Nation Goes to College*. National Panel Report. Washington, D.C.: Association of American Colleges and Universities, 2002. (ED 468 787)

Association of American Colleges and Universities. *College Learning for the New Global Century: A Report from the National Leadership Council for Liberal Education and America's Promise*. Washington, D.C.: Association of American Colleges and Universities, 2007. (ED 495 004)

Boyer, E. L. *College: The Undergraduate Experience in America.* New York: Harper and Row, 1987. (ED 279 259)

Doherty, A., Chenevert, J., Miller, R. R., Roth, J. L., and Truchan, L. C. "Developing Intellectual Skills." In J. G. Gaff, J. L. Ratcliff, and Associates (eds.), *Handbook of the Undergraduate Curriculum: A Comprehensive Guide to Purposes, Structures, Practices, and Change.* San Francisco: Jossey-Bass, 1997. (ED 401 816)

NANCY KINDELAN is an associate professor of theatre at Northeastern University.

NEW DIRECTIONS FOR TEACHING AND LEARNING • DOI: 10.1002/tl

5

This chapter introduces the theory and practice of work-based learning and provides guidelines for faculty with a particular emphasis on the value of reflective practice.

Work-Based Learning: Valuing Practice as an Educational Event

Joseph A. Raelin

The dominant method of providing formal knowledge to students in education in North America is through classroom training. The focus of this effort is on the delivery of a broad range of conceptual knowledge and skills in various liberal and professional fields of endeavor. Besides classroom instruction, the other predominant mode is through experience, whether through formal or informal assignments or placements. Through experience, students are able to obtain a truer forecast of the real world than when confined to a classroom. Unfortunately, classroom and real-world development experiences are typically provided independently, as if there were no need to merge theory with practice. Work-based learning, on the other hand, deliberately merges theory with practice and acknowledges the intersection of explicit and tacit forms of knowing at both individual and collective levels. It recognizes that learning is acquired in the midst of practice and can occur while working on the tasks and relationships at hand (Raelin, 2008).

As Wenger (1998) suggests, if we believe that knowledge is something that is stored, either in a library or in a brain, then it makes sense to package it and present it without distraction in a succinct and articulate way to receptive students. Knowledge acquisition would occur when it is transferred from the one who knows (the teacher or master) to the one who doesn't (the student or apprentice). What if we were to view knowledge, however, as something that is fluid, that can be created while we work together on exceptional, but also on mundane, work activities? Under this

NEW DIRECTIONS FOR TEACHING AND LEARNING, no. 124, Winter 2010 © Wiley Periodicals, Inc.
Published online in Wiley Online Library (wileyonlinelibrary.com) • DOI: 10.1002/tl.419

model, we would need to not only view the workplace as a suitable locus of learning, but create durable formats from which to draw contemporaneous lessons from experiences within the workplace.

Practice as an Educational Event

The word "practice" has many connotations; it can refer to a field of activity in which an individual works, or it can refer to the way that something is done or even to the repetition of an acquired skill. In this chapter, we are more concerned with its meaning as a method of learning and, in particular, its presence as an educational event. Thus, learning by practice signifies that it occurs more as a participative social process than as a phenomenon that takes place in a person's head. Therefore such learning is more likely to be as much collective as solitary, when people within a community share their everyday activities (Corradi, Gherardi, and Verzelloni, 2008).

What makes practice particularly noteworthy from an educational point of view is the opportunity it affords to promote new learning when we reach a point when we don't really know what to do (Cohen, 2007). As we plod along, searching for a way to "learn ourselves out," we may even find that our reliance on rationality may bog us down by overloading us with information or inflicting on us an "analysis paralysis" (Sadler-Smith and Shefy, 2007). Then, as Cunliffe (2002) reminds us in recalling Goethe, we may suddenly experience an "aperçu," a momentary insight that helps us convert our tacit knowledge in such a way that we entertain new possibilities.

Tacit Knowledge as the Gateway to Learning from Experience

Work-based learning can thus help us explore the tacit processes invoked personally by practitioners as they work through the problems of daily practice. According to Adaptive Character of Thought (ACT) Theory (Anderson, 1983), learning progresses through stages that approximate the cognitive architecture of memory. In the first cognitive stage, the learner acquires declarative knowledge, or a set of facts relevant to the skill in question, and processes this knowledge very deliberately. In the second association stage, the learner converts the declarative facts into procedural knowledge, which no longer requires the declarative information to be methodically retrieved into working memory. The transition from declarative to procedural knowledge has been referred to as the natural conversion from explicit to tacit knowledge or what Ryle (1949) referred to as moving from "knowing what" to "knowing how." For example, a novice learning to play the piano starts by locating the keys on the piano, but in time can make the transition to the tacit practice of playing the piano without even thinking of the keys. By the third, autonomous stage, as the skill becomes more and more automated, the learner is able to improve the search for new procedures and more efficiently transfer knowledge from one situation to the next.

As such, tacit knowledge is the component of knowledge that is not typically reportable since it is deeply rooted in action and involvement within a specific context (Polanyi, 1966). In other words, although individuals may be knowledgeable in what they do, they may not have the facility to say what it is they know (Pleasants, 1996). At this point, tacit knowledge may become intuitive—that is, we may have a sense of the correct action or response but may be incapable of explaining why we behaved the way we did (Gregory, 2000; Shirley and Langan-Fox, 1996). Yet, we seem able to quickly and effectively use this knowledge to handle ill-structured tasks, such as affirming a meaning to help us move towards problem resolution. In these instances, our information processing is often social, as we and others in our environment mutually build a knowledge base from the sharing of prior and current episodes or simply from our unique human awareness of our social and collective environment (Collins, 2007). At times in the "heat" of practice, often through dialogue with others, we improvise to maintain the flow of activity and, in so doing, refine and improve our practice (Gold, Thorpe, Woodall, and Sadler-Smith, 2007).

A critical issue for work-based learning, then, is not *whether* but *when* to introduce explicit instructions and reflection into the field to yield optimal performance. The construction of theory in this setting might be more apt during or after, rather than before, the experience. Hence, theory is not preordained but constituted as a living construction to capture the useful ingredients of the performance. In this sense, theory references the context from which it springs (Fish, 1989). Yet, there still remains the issue of how we surface contextual knowledge from our performance, even when it is masterful.

The Value of Reflective Practice

The tradition of reflective practice has a long history in classroom-based experiential education, though its contribution as a concurrent and collective practice supporting work experience is more recent (Raelin, 2001). There are a number of reasons for the late entry of this form of reflection into work-based educational activities. Prominent among these is the stark perspective, raised at the outset, that learning can occur in the midst of practice rather than more conventionally as a representation transmitted from teacher to student (Lave and Wenger, 1991). Instead of banking knowledge into one's mind (Freire, 1989), knowledge can be viewed as an interactive contention among a community of inquirers who share meanings, interpretations, and ideas.

From a contextualized learning perspective, reflective practice has a number of distinctive features that permit its consideration within the branch of learning referred to as *praxis*. First, it is not merely a cognitive or mental process but also a behavioral process. Second, it can involve others as opposed to being an individual experience. Third, it is typically concerned with critical inquiry, probing into the deep recesses of experience. Fourth, it can occur concurrently with practice rather than just before or after experience. Finally, it tends to require facilitation to help learners reframe their knowledge base. It thus calls for teachers to assume the role of the facilitator. Let's review some of these features.

Behavioral. That reflective practice can be a behavioral process suggests that learning can be more than representational; rather, it can refer to manifestations that though often cognitively derived are inherently behavioral, such as the ability to improvise or to point out connections among competing ideas. We also know that behavior can precede cognitive development or may be in continuous reciprocal interaction with cognitive and environmental influences (Vygotsky, 1962; Bandura, 1977).

Social/Collective. Although reflective practice can technically occur as a solitary process, it is frequently interactive, since most work entails contact with others. Further, though learners may reflect privately to compare phenomena against their cognitive frames, they often bring out their reflections with others once they become absorbed in practice. Their internal dialogue is enhanced by external dialogue that induces and then refines it (Wertsch, 1979). In other words, our experience with others informs us, pulls us, and even transforms us. As Wenger (1998) suggests, we create ways of learning in practice in the very process of contributing to making that practice what it is.

Reflective practice's interactive property resonated with Socrates, who had the idea of relationships in mind when he remarked that "the unexamined life is not worth living." This phrase has often been misinterpreted as a call for additional introspection. Although this misinterpretation can be a useful one, Socrates' actual meaning is that we need to include trusted others in the examination of experience in our lives. Socrates' idea, captured by Plato, resonated with Aristotle, who recognized that human beings are social animals whose individual good is bound up with the good of society. Jürgen Habermas (1984) saw the reconciliation between individual and society through intersubjective recognition based on mutual understanding and free cognition about disputed claims. It is through communicative action that we are able to realize ourselves within a civic community. We must subject our entire experience to criticism, even our tacit understanding.

Critical. Reflective practice's critical nature was taken up by Mezirow (1981), who referred to this level of discourse as "transformative," that is, a learning that can take us into new meanings. Transformative learning can help us review and alter any misconstrued meanings arising out of uncritical half-truths found in conventional wisdom or in power relationships. Mezirow (1991) later distinguished three forms of reflection based on the object of the reflection itself. *Content reflection* entails a review of the way we have consciously applied ideas in strategizing and implementing each phase of solving a problem. *Process reflection*, on the other hand, is an examination of how we go about problem-solving with a view toward the procedures and assumptions in use. *Premise reflection* goes to a final step of questioning the very presuppositions attending to the problem to begin with. In premise reflection, we question the very questions we have been asking in order to challenge our fundamental beliefs.

As a manifestation of critical inquiry, premise reflection takes into consideration data beyond our personal, interpersonal, and organizational taken-for-granted assumptions (Raelin, 1997). We need to understand how knowledge has been constructed and managed and how what is deemed to be relevant, or even commonsense, has been arrived at. For example, we may assume that everyone has the psychological and even physical security of opening up in front of others, but in fact this may not be the case for marginalized individuals or those untrained in the nuances of conversation. We need to elucidate the barriers preventing learners from finding their voices or reaching their potential (Shor, 1992). In finding their voices, participants learn to "speak up" in ways not just sanctioned by privileged social authorities but stemming from their self-identified interests.

Another way to view reflective practice's critical nature is to consider the form of knowledge to which the reflection may be dedicated. For example, we can refer to propositional knowledge, which involves placing into practice thoughtful action based on theoretical formulations (Grimmett and others, 1990). Propositional knowledge is concerned with "knowing what," while practical knowledge entails deliberation among competing versions of effective practice. The ensuing dialogue helps learners not just know what, but also "know how" (Sanders and McCutcheon, 1986).

A third form of knowledge is dialectical knowledge, which views reflection as the reorganization or reconstruction of experience. In this view, knowledge is emergent and viewed as a recasting or reframing of conventional ways of understanding so as to generate an appreciation of novelty in the practice situation (Grimmett and others, 1990). Dialectical knowledge can be used, therefore, to transform practice by asking practitioners to attend to features of the situation that were previously ignored. It might entail reconstructing taken-for-granted assumptions that might even lead the practitioner to identify and address the social, political, and cultural conditions that constrain self-insight (Habermas, 1971). It is concerned with not just knowing what and how, but with "knowing why."

Concurrent. Another important dimension of reflective practice is its time orientation. Adopting Loughran's labels (1996), anticipatory reflection occurs prior to experience, often in the form of planning as learners suggest to themselves and to their peers how they might approach a given situation. Retrospective reflection looks back at recent experience. It can be initiated as the first instance of reflection, or it may be triggered by plans and hypotheses generated from anticipatory reflection or by insights evolving from contemporaneous reflection.

Contemporaneous reflection occurs in the moment, akin to Schön's (1983) "reflection-in-action," such that in the midst of performance one reframes unanticipated problem situations in order to see an experience differently. While engaged in experience, planned responses often don't go according to plan, triggering a series of unexpected reactions. In this situation, the learner often reframes the problem on-the-spot in order to release oneself as well as one's colleagues from fixed views, leading to the consideration of new approaches.

Teacher as Facilitator. Learning requires facilitation not in a pure instructional sense but in a mediating sense. Bruner (1966) argued that instructors should engage students in active dialogue to help them discover principles by themselves. Facilitation models such behaviors as tolerance of ambiguity, openness and frankness, patience and suspension of judgment, empathy and unconditional positive regard, and commitment to learning. Hence, facilitators are interested less in teaching skills than in furnishing metacompetence—those principles that promote skill development across a range of circumstances. Facilitators also help learning teams engage in a constructive dialogue that is as free as possible from internal dynamics that may block productive discourse.

Teachers as facilitators stand back to allow learning to surface from the dialogue, emerging from experience. Therefore the teacher allows participants to offer their solutions to each other; admits fallibility along with a view on how everyone might approach the problem at hand, and invites participants to ask genuine questions to bring out the collective knowledge of all. In facilitating work-based experiences, teachers can also prepare students for ensuing practice or assist them in learning from their returning field placements.

Facilitation is most effective when attending to current experience, because it can assist participants in analyzing the process and outcomes of specific engagements and interventions. As Table 5.1 shows, such an analysis may incorporate five levels: Problem-Solving, Intellectual, Assumptive, Affective, and Critical (Qualters, 2008).

Conclusion

Work-based learning is mindful and situated learning in the sense that it does not view knowledge as fixed; rather knowledge is provisional until tried out in practice. It may also occur spontaneously rather than from memorizing and storing a range of facts to be used when needed. Learning is thus tied to practice, arising as people attempt to solve new and interesting problems, often improvising as they go. Work-based learning can be a refreshing and natural educational experience, especially when facilitated by engaged faculty.

NEW DIRECTIONS FOR TEACHING AND LEARNING • DOI: 10.1002/tl

Table 5.1. Analysis of Process and Outcomes

Level	Associated Questions
Problem-Solving	Did things go according to plan? What went well or only marginally well? What went badly? If a problem was solved, did it make a difference?
Intellectual	Were any puzzles or hypotheses presented? Were any contradictions or paradoxes revealed? Were any patterns revealed? Did any broader principles emerge?
Assumptive	What did you think was going to happen in this case? Were all assumptions tested for validity? What assumptions were borne out, were inaccurate?
Affective	What feelings or reactions were expressed? What feelings or reactions were not expressed and why? Were you empathic or judgmental and why?
Critical	Were the views of any involved party potentially excluded? Was there any expression of vulnerability? What prevented the speaker or others from solving the problem before?

Source: Adapted from Qualters, 2008.

References

Anderson, J. R. *The Architecture of Cognition*. Cambridge, MA: Harvard University Press, 1983.

Bandura, A. *Social Learning Theory*. New York: General Learning Press, 1977.

Bruner, J. S. *Toward a Theory of Instruction*. Cambridge, MA: Harvard University Press, 1966.

Cohen, M. D. "Reading Dewey: Reflections on the Study of Routine." *Organization Studies*, 2007, *28*(5), 773–786.

Collins, H. "Bicycling on the Moon: Collective Tacit Knowledge and Somatic-limit Tacit Knowledge." *Organization Studies*, 2007, *28*(2), 257–262.

Corradi, G., Gherardi, S., and Verzelloni, L. "Ten Good Reasons for Assuming a 'Practice Lens' in Organization Studies." Unpublished paper. Trento, Italy: Research Unit on Communication, Organizational Learning, and Aesthetics, University of Trento, 2008.

Cunliffe, A. L. "Reflexive Dialogical Practice in Management Learning." *Management Learning*, 2002, *33*(1), 35–61. (EJ 643 960)

Fish, S. *Doing What Comes Naturally: Change, Rhetoric, and the of Theory in Literary and Legal Studies*. Durham, NC: Duke University Press, 1989.

Freire, P. *Pedagogy of the Oppressed*. New York: Continuum, 1989. (ED 045 793)

Gold, J., Thorpe, R., Woodall, J., and Sadler-Smith, E. "Continuing Professional Development in the Legal Profession: A Practice-Based Learning Perspective." *Management Learning*, 2007, *38*(2), 235–250.

Gregory, G. "Developing Intuition Through Management Education." In T. Atkinson and G. Claxton (eds.), *The Intuitive Practitioner: On the Value of Not Always*

Knowing What One Is Doing. Buckingham, U.K.: Open University Press, 2000, pp. 182–195.

Grimmet, P. P., Erickson, G. L., Mackinnon, A. A., and Riecken, T. J. "Reflective Practice in Teacher Education." In R. T. Clift, W. R. Houston, and M. C. Pugach (eds.), *Encouraging Reflective Practice in Education: An Analysis of Issues and Programs*. New York: Teachers College Press, 1990, pp. 20–38.

Habermas, J. *Knowledge and Human Interests* (Trans. J. Shapiro). Boston: Beacon Press, 1971.

Habermas, J. *The Theory of Communicative Action. Volume 1: Reason and the Rationalization of Society* (Trans. T. McCarthy). Boston: Beacon Press, 1984.

Lave, J., and Wenger, E. *Situated Learning: Legitimate Peripheral Participation*. Cambridge, U.K.: Cambridge University Press, 1991.

Loughran, J. J. *Developing Reflective Practice: Learning about Teaching and Learning through Modelling*. London: Falmer Press, 1996.

Mezirow, J. "A Critical Theory of Adult Learning and Education." *Adult Education*, 1981, 32(1), 3–24. (EJ 253 326)

Mezirow, J. *Transformative Dimensions of Adult Learning*. San Francisco: Jossey-Bass, 1991. (ED 353 469)

Pleasants, N. "Nothing Is Concealed: De-centring Tacit Knowledge and Rules from Social Theory." *Journal for the Theory of Social Behaviour*, 1996, 26(3), 233–255.

Polanyi, M. *The Tacit Dimension*. Garden City, NY: Doubleday, 1966.

Qualters, D. M. "Engaging Faculty Colleagues in Experiential Education." Paper presented at the 2008 Martha's Vineyard Summer Institute on Experiential Education, Martha's Vineyard, MA, June 28, 2008.

Raelin, J. A. "A Model of Work-Based Learning." *Organization Science*, 1997, 8(6), 563–578.

Raelin, J. A. "Public Refection as the Basis of Learning." *Management Learning*, 2001, 32(1), 11–30. (EJ 623 914)

Raelin, J. A. *Work-Based Learning: Bridging Knowledge and Action in the Workplace*. San Francisco: Jossey-Bass, 2008.

Ryle, G. *The Concept of Mind*. Chicago: University of Chicago Press, 1949.

Sadler-Smith, E., and Shefy, E. "Developing Intuitive Awareness in Management Education." *Academy of Management Learning and Education*, 2007, 6(2), 186–205.

Sanders, D. P., and McCutcheon, G. "The Development of Practical Theories of Teaching." *Journal of Curriculum and Supervision*, 1986, 2(1), 50–67. (EJ 341 169)

Schön, D. A. *The Reflective Practitioner: How Professionals Think in Action*. New York: Basic Books, 1983.

Shirley, D. A., and Langan-Fox, J. "Intuition: A Review of the Literature." *Psychological Reports*, 1996, 79(2), 563–584.

Shor, I. *Empowering Education: Critical Teaching for Social Change*. Chicago: The University of Chicago Press, 1992. (ED 359 303)

Vygotsky, L. S. *Thought and Language*. Cambridge, M.A.: MIT Press, 1962.

Wenger, E. *Communities of Practice: Learning, Meaning, and Identity*. Cambridge, U.K.: Cambridge University Press, 1998.

Wertsch, J. V. "From Social Interaction to Higher Psychological Processes: A Clarification and Application of Vygotsky's Theory." *Human Development*, 1979, 22(1), 1–22. (EJ 208 451)

JOSEPH A. RAELIN is the Asa S. Knowles Chair of practice-oriented education at Northeastern University.

6

Students often face ethical challenges in experiential education. This chapter describes how teachers, supervisors, and administrators can help students circumvent "ethical bypassing" by strengthening practices of reflective ethical engagement and inquiry.

Empowering Reflective Ethical Engagement in Field Settings

Perrin Cohen

Intrinsic to experiential learning is the challenge of empowering students to both reflectively engage with and inquire into ethical issues, while facing time, task, social, and other daily pressures.

As designated "learners" in a professional setting, experiential education students typically see themselves as having little authority within the organization or group. This perception is commonly reinforced by others and undermines what would otherwise be their usual sense of moral authority and confidence. Students feel they do not have the right to express or share ethical concerns in such a setting, thinking "What do I know?" The result is that students often become ethically disempowered, disengaged, and passive even though they may sense that certain actions or procedures are "off" and need reflective attention and understanding. The pressures of expediency, distractions, and desensitization, as well as desires to succeed, fit in, and be acknowledged, strengthen habits of ethical complacency. I refer to such habits as "ethical bypassing" (Cohen, in preparation). Fortunately, ethical bypassing need not be part of a student's learning experience.

Ethical Concerns for Students

Before considering how to prepare students for reflective ethical engagement and inquiry, it is useful to consider the type and range of ethical concerns and pressures that students commonly encounter in their field

NEW DIRECTIONS FOR TEACHING AND LEARNING, no. 124, Winter 2010 © Wiley Periodicals, Inc.
Published online in Wiley Online Library (wileyonlinelibrary.com) • DOI: 10.1002/tl.420

work. Over the past fifteen years I have polled approximately 400 senior psychology majors in my *Ethics in Psychology* seminar about ethical issues that were challenging during their field work in clinics, classrooms, office, laboratories, and elsewhere. Table 6.1 summarizes the results of that poll. Even within a single major, it is clear that students experience a wide array of ethical challenges. The following are hypothetical examples that students are likely to encounter.

Example 1. On her first day on a community research project, Toby's supervisor gives her an overview of her responsibilities. An assistant then takes Toby on a tour of the facilities. When they enter the supply room, the assistant mentions that researchers and assistants are not allowed to use supplies for personal reasons but that "everyone does it." Toby is uneasy but decides that supplies are a fringe benefit.

Example 2. Sue works as a teacher's assistant in a preschool classroom as part of her internship. Johnny, one of the students, is the only boy in the class who likes to play with dolls. The teachers find it curious but don't give it much thought until Johnny's parents complain that it is "inappropriate." In an effort to accommodate Johnny's parents, the teachers remove all dolls from the playroom. Sue thinks that this is unfair but is uncomfortable discussing it with her supervising teachers. Although uncertain, she figures that must be the "professional" way to address the situation.

Learning to Forgo Ethical Bypassing

When students encounter ethical insensitivities, there is often little or no incentive, support, or preparation for establishing and maintaining a contemplative ethical perspective. The tendency is to react to these challenges with quick fixes that have worked in the past and leave students with a settled feeling that their actions are defensible under existing guidelines, rules, regulations, or laws. This "bypassing" maintains a comfort zone that allows students to efficiently meet deadlines, increase productivity, and avoid conflict, distractions, and personal dis-ease. Although bypassing provides quick relief in the short term, it ignores the longer-term risks of undermining trust, creating conflicts of interest and commitment, and adversely affecting reputation and well-being (Cohen, in preparation).

To help Northeastern University cooperative education students forgo ethical bypassing while they were in the workplace, we developed and taught both an Ethical Awareness on Co-op course and a related workshop for teachers (Cohen, McDaniels, and Qualters, 2005). The course and workshop were designed to empower students to take on the role of reflective ethical practitioner while they were under the pressures of being full-time employees. In taking on that role, students learned to bring reflective *awareness* and contextual sensitivity and mindfulness to ethical uneasiness, biases, assumptions, conflicts, and reactions in the workplace. That awareness served to "befriend" the ethical challenges, expand the student's field

NEW DIRECTIONS FOR TEACHING AND LEARNING • DOI: 10.1002/tl

Table 6.1. Some Areas and Examples of Ethical Challenge That Undergraduate Students Encounter

In Research	In Education	In the Clinic	In the Workplace
Research Misconduct/Honesty (data collection, analysis, interpretation, conflicts of interest, plagiarism, fraud)	Exploitation and Abuse of Student Athletes	Respect for Patient's Autonomy (nursing homes, informed consent, mental illness), Patient's Rights, and Health Care Providers' Autonomy	Lack of Supervision; Disregard for Rules and Guidelines
Research on Vulnerable Populations (prisoners, children, the disabled)	Roommates and Friends with Drug and Alcohol Problems, Eating Disorders	Socioeconomic Disparity and Cultural Incompetence in the Health Care System	Use and Misuse of Facebook
Fairness, Beneficence, and Use of Placebo Controls in Clinical Research	Achievement Gap and Testing in Public Schools; Distribution of Assets and Its Impact on Students and Teachers	Misuse/Overuse of Medications and Surgery (intersex, psychoactive medications for children, gene therapy, cosmetic surgery)	Unsafe Environments (toxic chemicals, physically abusive)
Animal Use (teaching, industry, species considerations)	Student Privacy, Values, Differences, and Personal Boundaries	Use and Misuse of Physical/Chemical Restraint, Diagnosis, and Testing	Use and Misuse of Drug Testing
Deception, Informed Consent, and Debriefing	Tracking and "Inclusion" in Special Education	Interviewing Children of Alleged Sexual Abuse	Gossip

Table 6.1. (Continued)

In Research	In Education	In the Clinic	In the Workplace
Obtaining Assent with Children Participants	Use and Misuse of Standardized Testing (College Admission)	Self Care in Helping Professions; Treatment of Elderly, Hospice Patients, Reunified Families	Pressures to Be Dishonest (on resumes, in job interviews, while completing tasks)
Authorship, Data Sharing, Editorial Review	Lack of Teacher Oversight, Knowledge, and Skill	Risks of Psychological and Crisis Interventions (behavioral therapies, punishment, suicide hotlines)	Inadequate Handling and Storage of Private Information
Controversial Research Protocols	Ethics in Teaching (teacher training, classroom)	Respect for Boundaries, Privacy, and Confidentiality in Clinical Settings; "Touching"	Discrimination (racism, sexism)
Using a Subject Pool	Cheating/Plagiarism	Confidentiality with AID/HIV Patients	Verbal Abuse
Genetic Engineering	Affirmative Action	Criminalization of Mental Illness; Involuntary Hospitalization	Sexual Harassment

of reflective *investigation* and reasoning, and provide a basis for practical *responding.*

Engagement Principles and Practices. Four engagement principles (Cohen, in preparation) guided those practices:

1. Proactively preserve and protect everyday conditions that support an attitude of goodwill toward oneself and others
2. "Befriend" rather than react to ethical concerns when they arise
3. Step back and critically assess *what can be known* both conceptually and contextually about ethical challenges
4. Make *plausible responses* to ethical challenges when and where appropriate.

In an earlier paper (Cohen, McDaniels, and Qualters, 2005), we qualitatively and quantitatively documented that these reflective practices and principles allow students to engage ethical concerns in the workplace.

Ethical Awareness on Co-op Course. One-credit courses called Ethical Awareness on Co-op were offered as free electives to Northeastern University students in four colleges (business, criminal justice, liberal arts, and health science) during the Spring Quarter 2002 and again during the Spring Quarter 2003. A total of eight courses were taught by eight different cooperative education co-coordinators who, prior to teaching, participated in a three-part teacher training seminar described below. Over the two-year period, a total of seventy students took the courses for eleven-week periods while concurrently working at their respective cooperative education jobs in the Boston area.

Learning Objectives and Ground Rules. The course was designed to help students learn to be reflective ethical practitioners. This involved learning to be mindful of workplace ethical concerns, to reflectively investigate concerns of particular interest, and to consider ways of converting ethical thinking into practical action when appropriate. Since daily pressures, distractions, and emotions readily disrupt these reflective practices, students and teachers agreed to create a safe context for such reflective inquiry. This was accomplished by agreeing on guidelines of confidentiality, active listening, and mutual respect.

Course Format. The course followed a hybrid in-class/online format. During the eleven-week quarter, students and teacher met as a group on campus in the evening during the third, seventh, and eleventh weeks of the course. Pizza and drinks were provided during the first half hour because students came directly from work. During the intervening weeks, students and teachers communicated online.

Sample Syllabus Topics. In the first two weeks of the course, students settled into their jobs. They reflectively discussed online the syllabus and readings chosen to introduce them to the role of reflective ethical practitioner. In the third week, students and teacher met in the classroom for the first time. The meeting covered introductions, course ground rules, grading, reading and resources, online procedures (for example, Blackboard, blog) and assignments, reflective ethical principles and practices, reflective ethical journaling (without jeopardizing work), and homework.

During the fourth, fifth, and sixth weeks of the course, students worked on online assignments involving detailed systematic deconstruction and discussion of ethical experiences. This included reflective discussion of context, underlying ethical concerns, personal feeling and thoughts, and outcomes. Students had a chance to share issues and experiences, both common and unique, across work settings. In the seventh week, the students and teacher met in the classroom for the second time for a follow-up discussion of journal entries. They explored reputable Internet resources (ethics centers, philosophy Web pages). Students chose one or two research tools or resources (ethical guidelines; stakeholders; duty-based analyses; cultural, psychological, sociological, spiritual/religious teachings; Web/university resources) to clarify and refine their ethical thinking. Students developed and discussed mini-research projects, such as investigating the strengths and limitations of professional guidelines in a particular work setting or doing a stakeholder or cost/benefit analysis of a particular ethical concern.

During the eighth, ninth, and tenth weeks of the semester, students continued their online assignments and discussions, which covered the use of research tools, ethical guidelines, journaling, communication skills, and research projects. In the eleventh and final week, the students and teacher met in the classroom for the last time. Students submitted and discussed their mini-research reports. Further discussion covered the identification of common themes and issues across workplace settings, course feedback, next steps, and the risks and benefits of taking on the role of reflective ethical practitioner.

Teacher Training Seminar. We developed and team-taught a three part teacher training seminar that prepared teachers to teach the Ethical Awareness on Co-op course. The seminar was completed by eight Northeastern University cooperative education co-coordinators prior to teaching the course. They received extra remuneration for participating in the seminar and only taught students in their specialty areas.

Learning Objectives and Ground Rules. The seminar was designed to help co-coordinators empower students to reflectively engage with and inquire into ethical concerns in their work setting. Co-coordinators practiced reflective ethical practices and principles in "student"/teacher role plays. They also practiced using guidelines and developed syllabi for their courses.

Course Format. The seminar met once a week for a half day over three successive weeks prior to offering the courses.

Sample Syllabus Topics. The first meeting provided an overview of course rationale, ground rules, and sample readings. Co-coordinators shared professional ethical experiences and ethical concerns expressed by students and discussed types of ethical bypassing, how to deconstruct and discuss an ethical concern, and Internet issues and applications. At the second meeting, co-coordinators discussed their homework projects and ethical scenarios. They participated in "student"/teacher role-playing exercises. The meeting covered practical resources, practices, principles, and tools for cultivating reflective ethical engagement and inquiry. In the final meeting, co-coordinators reviewed the practices and material covered in the previous meeting. They discussed communication skills, online and in-class formats, and the difference between "giving advice" to students and supporting reflective ethical inquiry. Each co-coordinator developed their Web site structure and course syllabus.

Summary and Conclusions

Experiential education students encounter many types of ethical concerns in their field settings but usually have little or no incentive, support, or preparation for addressing them in a contemplative way. More often than not, they "bypass" them with quick fixes that preserve their comfort zone but ignore the longer-term risks to themselves and others. The two courses described allow teachers to empower experiential education students to strengthen practices of reflective ethical engagement and inquiry. The concepts, principles, and pedagogical methods used in these courses can readily be adapted in whole or in part to other types of experiential education settings (Cohen, McDaniels, and Qualters, 2005; Cohen and Qualters, 2007).

The primary challenge that we faced in implementing these courses was finding *consistent* administrative support. Some administrators and colleagues readily supported the goal of cultivating reflective ethical engagement and inquiry in a field setting and saw it as a core institutional and educational objective. They saw our work as a priority due to the many ethical challenges that students encounter in the field. For them, the courses were a prototype for future innovation and for reconsidering ethical awareness and leadership (Cohen and Qualters, 2007) within a field setting.

Most colleagues, however, had a different and conflicting perspective. In spite of the documented effectiveness of the courses, they felt students received adequate preparation for facing routine ethical uncertainties with exposure to ethical compliance (laws, ethical guidelines) and with ad hoc course work (moral philosophy courses, textbook chapters, occasional class discussions). From this perspective, they saw no need to support ethical contemplation within a field setting as a core educational objective. This latter view eventually prevailed and the course and seminar described in this chapter were discontinued after two years.

I expect that with a greater awareness of how "ordinary" ethical complacency adversely affects our environment, the global economy, technology, and medicine, mainstream educators will begin to appreciate the need to educate students to reflectively pause, acknowledge, and investigate ethical concerns and uncertainties in everyday situations. The flexibility and autonomy inherent in field settings, experiential learning, and distance learning provide ready opportunities for that. Hopefully, the ethical practitioner approach and related courses outlined in this chapter are an impetus and framework for moving in that direction.

References

Cohen, P. "A Practitioner Model for Ethical Leadership." *Academic Leader*, June 2007, 23(6), 6–8.
Cohen, P. "Maintaining Your Ethical Bearings." Manuscript in preparation.
Cohen, P., McDaniels, M. and Qualters, D. M. "AIR Model: A Teaching Tool for Cultivating Reflective Ethical Inquiry." *College Teaching*, 2005, 54(3), 120–127. (EJ 725 829)
Cohen, P., and Qualters, D. M. "Ethical Leadership: The AIR Model Empowers Moral Agency." *Journal of Human Values*, 2007, 13(2), 107–117.

Acknowledgments

A special thanks to my collaborators, Donna Qualters and Melissa McDaniels, and to Sandra Meyer Cohen for her support and feedback in developing these teaching programs. I also thank David Hall for his important contributions.

PERRIN COHEN *is an associate professor of psychology and founder and director of Northeastern University's Ethics Education Center (NUCASE).*

7

Assessment is often seen as punitive, difficult, or irrelevant to real learning. But viewed differently, assessment can be a valuable tool to foster growth in experiential learning.

Bringing the Outside In: Assessing Experiential Education

Donna M. Qualters

Mention the word assessment to faculty colleagues and they probably will share strong opinions from "it's a bean-counting waste of time" to "I'd love to but I don't have time or skills." In this chapter I hope to change that particular view of assessment and share some practical techniques to engage faculty in the process of gaining valuable information to improve student learning in experiential education.

The topic raises the question: What does assessment mean in experiential education? Is it evaluation? Is it formal or informal? Is perceptual data assessment? Do I need a rigorous design methodology? The practical answer to all of these questions is "possibly." There are many reasons to assess and many different lenses through which to look at assessment. For the purposes of this chapter, we will define assessment using Barbara Walvoord's practical definition: "Assessment of student learning is the systematic gathering of information about student learning and the factors that affect learning, undertaken with the resources, time and expertise available, for the purpose of improving learning" (Walvoord, 2009).

The experiential education process on many campuses can be viewed in Exhibit 7.1. What is missing in this cycle is the opportunity to document the power and the learning of the experience. As stated in previous chapters, experiential education is not just integration of theory and practice but can (and should) be transformative, creating new knowledge, skills, and attitudes for students that neither theory nor practice alone can accomplish. If colleges and universities want to engage in meaningful experiential

NEW DIRECTIONS FOR TEACHING AND LEARNING, no. 124, Winter 2010 © Wiley Periodicals, Inc.
Published online in Wiley Online Library (wileyonlinelibrary.com) • DOI: 10.1002/tl.421

Figure 7.1. Experiential Education on Many College Campuses

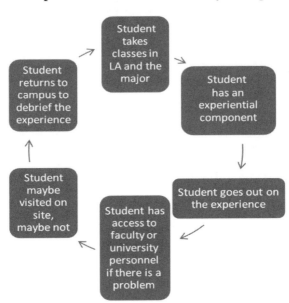

education, they need to find ways to capture this transformation and to use this data to continually document, explain, and improve experiential education activities.

To do this, it is important to look at assessment as more than an outcome measurement. While outcomes are important to measure, they reflect the end product of assessment, not a complete assessment cycle. Outcomes of experiential education are also difficult to measure as there are many confounding variables that make this challenging, such as student maturation, preexperience anxiety, and demographics (Ewert and Sibtorp, 2009). Sandra Elman, Executive Director of the Commission on Colleges of the Northwest Association of Schools and Colleges, has discussed four "essential questions" that campuses need to seriously discuss before they conceive of an assessment design (see Figure 7.2) (Elman, 1993).

The power of these questions resides in the campus-wide involvement and discussion from various perspectives that is needed to fully answer these questions and to create comfort and buy-in for all participants. Answering these questions about experiential education accomplishes multiple outcomes. First, they focus faculty on the big pictures of experiential education assessment as involving many facets of the campus. Second, to answer the questions one must think carefully about the details of the experience. Third, they provide the opportunity to look at multiple methods, as discussions will raise questions that require a variety of data-

Figure 7.2. Four Essential Questions

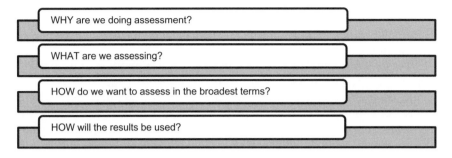

WHY are we doing assessment?

WHAT are we assessing?

HOW do we want to assess in the broadest terms?

HOW will the results be used?

Source: Adapted from Elman, 1993.

gathering approaches. Lastly, they provide transparency about assessment. One of the biggest concerns I have heard expressed by faculty about assessment is the usage of the data gathered through the process. By engaging faculty, staff, students, site personnel, and community members in answering these questions, the fears that come with change and new ideas are addressed early and clearly.

The next helpful step is to engage in the activity of answering what Paloma and Banta (1999) call "burning questions." These are the questions that all parties involved in the experiential experience are really concerned about answering. For example, faculty may be concerned with capturing whether or not students are using classroom theory in practice; students may wonder how the experience enhances their discipline knowledge; administrators may be concerned with how accreditation will view these activities; staff may be apprehensive about the processes involved in setting up the activity; and the site personnel may be anxious about how the student involvement affects their clients. By eliciting burning questions, you can develop and prioritize assessment mechanisms to provide useful answers, not just accumulate data that only a small group is concerned about using.

This leads us to the next step: separating the types of assessment and organizing the approach in a systematic way. When we talk about experiential education and assessment, we are talking about two different types of assessment. The first, program assessment, is probably the easiest and the most common type of assessment. Experiential program assessment is often about quantitative numbers, such as number of student participants, grade point averages of students, postgraduation work, and so forth. Most of the data is external and collectable. It is important information about the overall success of experiential education programming.

However, experiential education is also about experiential learning, and that involves learning assessment, which can be much more difficult to measure. However, the degree of difficulty should not discourage this type of assessment, as the real purpose of assessment is to provide meaningful data to improve learning.

Before discussing "how to," we need to address another consideration in learning assessment: faculty engagement in the process. While there are faculty on every campus involved in experiential education, engaging them in assessing the learning these experiences create can be more difficult. To assess learning acquired during an experience often requires probing qualitatively as well as quantitatively into student learning processes. The result of understanding the student learning process could suggest a change in teaching methodology. Trigwell and Prosser (1996) demonstrated that faculty often make changes in teaching practices based on their concept of the role of a teacher and their perception of the match between the new idea and their internal belief system. To engage faculty in the experiential assessment process means to understand how your faculty view the experiential education and what role they see themselves playing in the experience. To do this, provide longitudinal venues such as dialogue groups (Qualters, 2000), faculty learning communities, or semester-long brown bag discussions. A good idea is to invite two faculty members from a department or division to participate, as this will provide cohort support when going back to a department to encourage assessment. Learning assessment is most meaningful when the faculty are active participants in designing the process and reviewing the products of learning.

Measuring Learning

Clearly assessment is complex, but at the same time it needs to be accessible to faculty. Some of the elements of good assessment are universal and already in use. Most experiential education situations result in student feedback (perceptual data); site feedback (perceptual data); and grades (quantitative measurement). However, to gather valuable data about learning during an experience, we must understand the process of the learning; we must reflect on it and reorganize the learning to make students aware of what they have actually learned and how it connects with previous learning and discipline theory. None of the methods above will accomplish this.

While there are many models of assessment, in order to meet the twin goals of assessing learning and engaging faculty in the process I am revisiting a classic model. In 1993, Alexander Astin put forth an elegant assessment model that can be easily adapted to experiential education. Astin's model, referred to as I–E–O, possesses all the elements that make it adaptable and useful for experiential education. In this model, I equals *input*, that is, assessing students before an intervention, finding students' current knowledge, skills and attitudes. E is *environment*, which means assessing students during the experience; and O is *output*, assessing the success after the experience.

Practical Applications. Below is an example using this model. In an allied health field, students were being placed in the community to do health education with the homeless population. Prior traditional methods of conducting surveys yielded postexperience euphoria (Ewert and Sibthorp, 2009). After the experience, student responses were mostly impressive in what many students claimed to have learned about health education and working with a homeless population. The dilemma from a programmatic view was documenting the actual cognitive and affective learning while also improving the experience for students, the community site, and the homeless population it served. From a learning perspective, the issue became how to separate perceived learning from genuine learning and how to begin to capture that growth and change. Working together through the steps listed above, the faculty was able to articulate what they wanted, how they might do it, and how the data would be used. They then identified the "burning questions" they wanted to answer about this experience. Lastly, with the help and guidance of a learning specialist, they applied the I–E–O model and developed the following design.

I   Before students went into the community, they were surveyed on their attitudinal assumptions. They were asked about their conceptions of the community with which they would be interacting; their concerns about going into the community; and what they wanted to gain from the experience. They were then put through a mini observed structured clinical experience (OSCE) to have concrete evidence of their skill level.

E   During the experience students kept structured reflective journals and engaged in collective reflection. They also had periodic structured observations from faculty on the growth of their knowledge and skill in the community setting.

O   After the experience, the students were given the same survey of attitudes to identify changes. They were asked to identify any new insights they might now have about community health, or working with the homeless population; or any thoughts they had about doing health education in the community. They were also put through the OSCE again.

While not a perfect model, it did provide some very valuable assessment data. First, it allowed a true assessment of skill development with no confounding variable, as the community was the only site where students practiced blood pressure and interviewing. More importantly, the observations, journal, and collective reflections allowed the faculty to understand student learning processes as skills improved and attitudes evolved. By adding the pre- and postexperience surveys, faculty were able to surface student attitudes and misconceptions prior to going into the community, an important step in addressing and structuring the experience to prove or disprove their beliefs (Wiggins and McTighe, 2005).

This survey revealed the misconceptions (and fears) students had about working with the homeless, which allowed faculty in subsequent course iterations to add this important element to their students' preparation before entering the community and to ask students to journal about their feelings and perceptions as they worked alongside the homeless. It also provided the initial baseline data for faculty to determine whether their subsequent interventions actually reduced misconceptions. Lastly, it provided triangulation of data as students identified new ideas, insights, and procedure suggestions that demonstrated a much deeper understanding than just observation and testing showed. Faculty could understand how the students were thinking, direct their reflection to make connections with prior knowledge and theory, and help them identify new insights as they reflected through writing and in groups. This method met the criteria for good assessment: It was ongoing, aimed at improving *and* understanding learning, had public and explicit expectations, set appropriate standards, and was used to document, explain, and improve performance (Angelo, 1995). But it also seemed reasonable, doable, and logical to the faculty, as it drew on methods and models of the discipline as well as educational methodologies.

In subsequent iterations, faculty used an adaptation of Nuhfer and Knipp's Knowledge Survey (1991). This survey is a series of questions designed around the area of the experience. The questions are categorized along Bloom's taxonomy to ensure higher-level thinking is addressed and not just rote recall. The purpose of the survey is not to test student knowledge but to provide a study guide that discloses the organization, content, and level of thinking expected in the experience. Students are told that it is a device to help them monitor their own growth through the experience. In the original method, students do not answer questions; rather, they mark their confidence level in each question. If they are confident in their answer they mark A; if they feel they know part of the answer but could easily find the needed information they mark B; and if they are not confident at all in the answer they mark C. This survey was administered before and after, and added the affective component to measure confidence, which has been shown to parallel the ability to address the question in an exam setting.

Putting It All Together

One of the most comprehensive methods of assessing experiential learning is the learning portfolio. What distinguishes a learning portfolio from a professional portfolio is the reflection component. A learning portfolio is not just a showcase of student materials, but a purposefully designed collection connected by carefully thought out structured student reflections. Portfolios take time to develop the content, structure the reflective writings, and develop the rubrics for reviewing them; it can be challenging, but the benefit far outweighs the challenges, as these portfolios serve many masters. Well-constructed portfolios can be used for accreditation purposes, for college-wide outcome assessment, for departmental and course-specific understanding of the process of learning, and to document the affective component of the experiential activity. In other words, they can help answer not only administrative and externally driven assessment questions but also (and perhaps more importantly) faculty-driven burning questions about the experiential learning in their course, department, or division. The advent of open source ware makes this an inexpensive option as well.

Conclusion

In assessment, there are no conclusions, just ongoing questions that the data raise about learning and the process of learning. To make assessment of experiential education meaningful, it must meet multiple agendas and consist of many different methods of capturing the learning. But it need not be complex or held to the standard used when publishing data; that level will only be perceived as time-consuming and low-priority by many faculty. With a clear consideration of design that goes beyond perceptions into documenting learning, by developing new tools to capture praxis and by using a multipronged approach that engages faculty in identifying and designing methods to answer their burning questions, experiential education can move from the periphery of learning to demonstrating that learning beyond the classroom is a central component of education in higher education.

References

Angelo, T. A. "Reassessing (and Defining) Assessment: A Second Try." *AAHE Bulletin*, 1995, *48*(3).
Astin, A. *Assessment for Excellence*. Phoenix: The Oryx Press, American Council on Education Series on Higher Education, 1993.
Elman, S. "Outcome Assessment." Presentation to the faculty of Endicott College, Beverly, MA. March 1993.
Ewert, A., and Sibthorp, J. "Creating Outcomes Through Experiential Education: The Challenge of Confounding Variables." *Journal of Experiential Education*, 2009, *31*(3), 376–389. (EJ 853 338)
Nuhfer, E. and Knipp, D. "The Knowledge Survey: A Tool for All Reasons." In C. Wehlburg and S. Blossey (eds.), *To Improve the Academy: Resources for Faculty, Instructional, and Organizational Development*, vol. 21. Bolton, MA: Anker Publishing Company, 2003.
Palomba, C. A., and Banta, T. W. *Assessment Essentials: Planning, Implementing, and Improving Assessment in Higher Education*. San Francisco: Jossey-Bass, 1999. (ED 430 507)
Qualters, D. M. "Creating Faculty Community." *The National Teaching Learning Forum*, May 2000, *9*(4), 1–6.

Trigwell, K. and Prosser, M. "Towards an Understanding of Individual Acts of Teaching." Paper presented at the 1996 Higher Education Research and Development Society of Australasia. Retrieved December 21, 2009, from www.herdsa.org.au/ confs/1996/trigwell1.html.

Walvoord, B. "Reflection on Assessment in Departments and General Education: How to Be More Realistic, Effective, and Time-Efficient." Paper presented at the 2009 New Association of Schools and Colleges (NEASC) Annual Meeting. Boston, December 2009.

Wiggins, G., and McTighe, J. *Understanding by Design*. Alexandra, VA: Association for Supervision and Curriculum Development, 2005. (ED 424 227)

DONNA M. QUALTERS *is the director of the Center for Teaching Excellence and an associate professor of education at Suffolk University.*

8

This chapter describes ways in which institutions can develop thriving experiential learning programs despite challenging economic times. Stage-specific challenges and cost-effective solutions are outlined.

Growing and Funding Experiential Learning Programs: A Recipe for Success

Monica R. Cowart

While numerous professors and administrators can agree upon the benefits of infusing the curriculum with experiential learning (Higgins, 2009; Cheek and others, 2007; Beard and Wilson, 2006), a commonly stated obstacle to widespread curricular reform is funding. Specifically, given that external institutional support can be difficult to procure, especially in uncertain economic times, institutions might question whether it makes sense to start experiential learning initiatives, especially if long-term funding is uncertain. While, ideally, initiating an experiential learning program would involve allocating ample funds for faculty development grants and professional development programs, it is incorrect to assume that this is the *only* model that will result in a flourishing experiential learning program.

This chapter provides an alternative model to extensive internal funding streams by outlining how a college or university with limited resources can find the internal and external resources to start or enhance an experiential learning program. Using Merrimack College, a small tuition-dependent liberal arts college north of Boston, as a case study, this chapter will discuss the specific challenges programs can face when trying to find the resources to incorporate experiential learning initiatives into their curriculum. For each challenge that is identified, specific strategies are provided to successfully address that challenge. Moreover, challenges and solutions are provided from multiple perspectives (students, faculty, and administrative challenges) so that a comprehensive strategic plan is formulated that

NEW DIRECTIONS FOR TEACHING AND LEARNING, no. 124, Winter 2010 © Wiley Periodicals, Inc.
Published online in Wiley Online Library (wileyonlinelibrary.com) • DOI: 10.1002/tl.422

includes the perspectives of all stakeholders. Finally, these challenges and tested solutions are articulated within a larger "developmental" framework, which traces the funding challenges and solutions experiential learning programs can encounter as they grow over time. The chapter concludes with specific lessons learned from the Merrimack College case study, but the overall chapter will aim to broadly suggest strategies that other colleges can use to address funding challenges.

Merrimack College

In less than ten years, Merrimack College has progressed from a novice experiential learning (EL) institution to an institution poised to transcend to integrated status. This process started with a core group of faculty who were committed to seeing EL grow from a handful of courses to a shared pedagogical vision in which EL is integrated across the curriculum. Current EL initiatives are (1) highlighted in college brochures and alumni magazines, (2) funded through internal and external grants, and (3) showcased in one of two possible new general education programs. Given this progression, one might ask: How was Merrimack College able to progress from no coordinated EL efforts to its current status? Yet the more interesting question is: How was the college able to achieve this end despite the lack of initial resources?

Developmental Stages and Strategic Plan Development

The challenges associated with EL programs will vary depending upon the developmental stage of the program in question. While particular programs should be considered as existing on a developmental continuum, for our purposes, we will examine growing EL programs from inception (novice) to acceptance (integrated). By explaining each category and its accompanying challenges, institutional planning committees can produce strategic plans that anticipate appropriate growth and proactive problem-solving. Let's consider each program type and the corresponding challenges.

Novice EL Programs

A novice program is any program that does not have a formal institutionalized mechanism for delivering EL. In other words, there is not an EL office, no budget, nor staff members who are devoted to furthering EL initiatives on campus. Instead, EL courses might exist on campus, but they are provided by faculty members who believe in these pedagogical practices and continue to deliver these courses, despite the lack of institutional support. In addition, cooperative education or service-learning opportunities might exist, but there is no coordinated effort in terms of mission or vision that unites these various efforts. A novice EL "program" is born when faculty

NEW DIRECTIONS FOR TEACHING AND LEARNING • DOI: 10.1002/tl

and administrators who are individually delivering these opportunities find one another and suggest coordinating efforts. These individuals might form a formal or informal campus group to explore the development of an official EL program on their campus. The goal of a novice program is to create an institutionalized mechanism for delivering EL opportunities, given that the college is not yet valuing, or simply does not have the resources to finance, these types of experiences. One of the biggest challenges for a novice program is to try to convince others, particularly students, of the value of EL.

Student Challenges and Solutions. Students often view EL courses as more time-intensive than "regular" versions of the same courses. They want to know why taking an EL course is worth their time and effort. The key to achieving student support is to demonstrate that course content becomes more relevant, meaningful, and clearly understood when an EL format is used. Once students recognize that the EL process provides unique opportunities to link theory and practice, they are more likely request EL courses.

The solution to this challenge is creating venues in which students are aware of the current EL opportunities on campus as well as the benefits they provide. Since students tend to respond more readily to first-hand accounts by their peers who have already had an EL course, having student-driven panel discussions, student-made videos, or student-run campus events that publicize recent EL initiatives can help to increase student interest. This, in turn, can lead to student-driven requests for more EL courses. Faculty and administrators also should be invited to these events so that they can see the positive impact these initiatives have on students.

Faculty Challenges and Solutions. Faculty members who have never taught EL courses often question whether implementing EL will be worth the extra effort required to learn new techniques and update courses. These individuals might describe the process as "too daunting" or "too difficult" to undertake without a faculty development grant. Still other faculty might argue that EL is "not really teaching" and might claim that it is not pedagogically sound. The strategy to address these concerns is twofold: (1) recognize that faculty who are new to EL will need the support of more experienced faculty who are already engaged in the process, and (2) share the outcome-based literature on EL, which demonstrates that this approach enhances the educational experience.

While students respond more to personal accounts, faculty members should be shown the growing literature that conveys the advantages of incorporating EL into the curriculum. One solution for helping those faculty members who are interested yet overwhelmed by the process is to start an EL support group and mentoring program. Experienced EL faculty members can be paired with faculty members who are contemplating offering a course. The mentoring relationship can help to diminish the anxiety that can accompany the initial offering of an EL course. In addition, a monthly support group of faculty members can offer individuals a forum to strategize, problem-solve, and build community around EL issues. Again, these efforts to raise faculty awareness of EL successes can be achieved with minimal resources.

Administrative Challenges and Solutions. Administrators might recognize that EL courses are effective ways of helping students make stronger connections between theory and practice, but in tough economic times they might rationalize that standard methods of course delivery are "good enough." Therefore, the challenge for a novice program is acquiring resources from the administration in order to fund a centralized EL office, so that further support is provided to faculty and students. After faculty support and student demand for courses have increased, then an argument can be advanced to the administration that developing an official EL program on campus that coordinates efforts will help attract new students and aid in retention of current students. Specifically, admission and retention arguments that connect with the now-growing grassroots demand for courses can result in the administration offering funding for a pilot program, a part-time staff member to coordinate efforts, or development money to attend an EL Institute in order to learn to develop a campus-wide strategic plan.

Integrated EL Programs

An integrated program is any program that has (1) a visible degree of student support and faculty delivery of EL courses, (2) a formal institutionalized mechanism for advancing EL initiatives (formal committee, campus office), and (3) some level of funding devoted to strengthening these programs. An integrated program builds upon all of the grassroots efforts that defined a novice program, but the central difference is that the EL initiatives of integrated programs are formally supported by the college or university. The degree of support, especially in difficult economic times, might vary from institution to institution, but in each case the inherent value of the EL program is recognized by the institution. Once an EL program has progressed to the integrated stage, a host of new challenges surface—including the necessity of providing consistency and preventing burnout—which require equally innovative solutions.

Student Challenges and Solutions. As programs transition from novice to integrated status, there reaches a point in which multiple forms of EL courses are offered from professors with a variety of experience levels. One consequence is that students might complain that courses have inconsistent standards for what counts as EL, resulting in some courses being more rigorous than others. One way to address this challenge is to establish a formal EL committee to develop school-wide criteria to which a course must adhere in order for it to carry the EL designation. For instance, the committee might decide that courses must involve a written reflection on the EL and that the EL component must be directly connected with the course content. Consequently, the committee would reject Professor X's request to offer his engineering course with an EL designation, since he mistakenly thought that requiring his students to hand out meals at a homeless shelter would qualify. Again, the EL committee can pull from the existing academic literature to adopt and refine a campus-wide definition of EL that will enable them to create minimal criteria that must be met for courses to carry an EL designation.

Faculty and Administrative Challenges and Solutions. As EL becomes more integrated into the curriculum and administrators begin to see its benefits, additional demands can be made on the core group of EL faculty who started these efforts, such as being asked to speak with prospective students, explaining their projects at alumni fundraising efforts, or mentoring additional interested faculty. Since a lack of funding in addition to increased demands on time can quickly lead to burnout, it is important to find ways in which experienced EL faculty can support these growing efforts without expecting them to singlehandedly carry these programs. One cost-effective solution is to have the core EL faculty rotate these responsibilities, or have members divide the work according to subcommittees. For instance, one member might agree to speak at all fundraising events, while another member will choose instead to mentor faculty who are new to EL. However, it should be noted that once a program has grown to the integrated stage of development, there should be enough support on campus to warrant pursuing internal and external funding sources that are supported by the institution. For instance, exciting EL initiatives can be showcased in the alumni magazine or included in a capital campaign.

Formalized Strategic Plan and Grants

Once top administrators and faculty recognize that they want EL to be part of their institution's long-range, pedagogical vision, it is time to formally include EL in institutional planning. If the institution currently offers faculty development grants for research and teaching, then these categories can be expanded to fund EL course development. In addition, an EL grant writing committee can be formed to explore possible regional and national teaching grants that can be written with an EL focus. One might write a three-year grant proposal that would pay for release time from teaching so that faculty members can develop new EL courses, or release time so that advanced EL faculty can mentor novice faculty. Ideally, grants should be written with a two- to three-year timetable so that there will be a few years of externally funded program stability before a new funding stream needs to be pursued.

Lessons Learned: Revisited

As a member of the initial EL committee and subsequent grant writing committee, the most surprising part of this process occurred when our

NEW DIRECTIONS FOR TEACHING AND LEARNING • DOI: 10.1002/tl

program was in the novice stage of development. Specifically, I am amazed at what a small group of committed individuals was able to achieve, despite the lack of initial funding. By the time this chapter is published, our faculty senate will have voted on whether to add an EL component to our general education program. Regardless of the outcome, our campus has moved from a time when only a select few had even heard of EL to a time when faculty are debating about whether every student must take an EL course in order to graduate. Regardless of the outcome of the senate motion, I consider this a success story.

References

Beard, C., and Wilson, J. P. *Experiential Learning: A Best Practice Handbook for Educators and Trainers* (2nd ed.). London: Kogan Page, 2006.

Cheek, T., Rector, K., and Davis, C. "The Clothesline Project: An Experiential Learning Project with MSW Students." *Journal of Teaching in Social Work*, 2007, 27(1/2), 141–154.

Higgins, Peter. "Into the Big Wide World: Sustainable Experiential Learning Education for the 21st Century." *Journal of Experiential Education*, 2009, 32(1), 44–60.

MONICA R. COWART is chairperson of and an associate professor in the Philosophy Department at Merrimack College.

9

Campus implementation of experiential education can seem daunt-ing. This chapter shares three case studies of successful implemen-tation at very different types of institutions.

Campus Stories: Three Case Studies

Part A: Institutionalizing Pedagogical Change: A Case Study in Building a Learning Organization

Victoria A. Farrar-Myers, Dana Dunn

In response to the growing calls for accountability in higher education, accreditation associations are requiring institutions to develop strategic plans designed to enhance student learning. This requirement can be recast as a unique opportunity to promote institution-wide introspection and col-laboration. Such a plan can foster an open dialogue among all the stake-holders of the university regarding the direction they want the institution to take and the learning they wish their students to achieve. The key to tak-ing advantage of this opportunity is developing a mindset throughout the university that emphasizes the plan and its development as a catalyst to bring the university together with a renewed sense of community.

To make the plan a catalyst for long-term institutional change, the institution itself must be treated as a learning organization. All the mecha-nisms of learning that we seek to promote among our students should be employed in creating the plan: brainstorming, making connections between disparate ideas, understanding the implications of decisions, and decon-structing information and building it back up in a new and more useful way. This case study examines the lessons learned from the University of Texas at Arlington (UT Arlington) 2006–2007 experience to identify sev-eral key principles—how to build a stakeholder-driven process, how to develop constructive working relationships, and how to create a learning

NEW DIRECTIONS FOR TEACHING AND LEARNING, no. 124, Winter 2010 © Wiley Periodicals, Inc.
Published online in Wiley Online Library (wileyonlinelibrary.com) • DOI: 10.1002/tl.423

organization—required to institutionalize active learning, experiential education, and the shared vision to achieve the desired educational outcomes (UT Arlington, 2007).

The Keys to Success

Our process of institutionalizing pedagogical change started with two fundamental questions: (1) What kind of educational experience do we want our students to have? and (2) What do we want our students to learn? The answers would enable us to identify the desired educational outcomes. Just as important as answering these questions, though, was the *process* by which they were answered. In our case, the university leadership was committed to an open, stakeholder-driven process in which the various constituencies of the university, particularly the faculty, were given multiple opportunities to participate in shaping the answers to these questions. Only after the academic community's desires were identified and defined could the process of change begin.

From this experience, three keys to fostering change emerged. First, university leaders need to understand and take advantage of the culture of the university and its various constituencies. Second, they must be deliberate in the model of institutionalization employed. Finally, there must be an intentionality of design in developing the learning instrument(s) used. Moreover, these keys to change must be integrated so that efforts in one area complement and build upon the other areas.

University Culture and Subcultures. UT Arlington's culture can be summarized in one word: diversity. Composed of ten colleges and schools, UT Arlington is a large, urban university with more than 28,000 students. It has a strong history in teaching across a wide array of academic disciplines and a strong-college model of governance. The university, however, is a "research university with high research" (RU/H, in the Carnegie Foundation's Classification of Institutions of Higher Education), and aspires to be a "research university with very high research" (RU/VH). Efforts to institutionalize pedagogical change such as active learning and experiential education must be sensitive to the existence of this dual teaching and research culture. Failure to consider both sets of interests runs the risk of alienating a large number of faculty and students who feel their interests are not being addressed. Furthermore, within the university, each of the various academic units had their own set of interests, concerns, vocabulary, and approaches—in effect, their own subcultures—that needed to be taken into account. Any approach to university-wide pedagogical change would need to address these subcultures.

The student body also reflects the diversity of the metropolitan area in which it is situated (UT Arlington, 2007, pp. 4–5). Most students (58%) are between the ages of 18–24, yet the university has historically drawn and continues to draw many nontraditional-aged students as well. The diversity of the student body is also seen in the large percentage of Hispanics (14%), African Americans (12%), Asian Americans (11%), and international students (11%) attending the university. A majority of our students (54%) are women. The academic achievement levels of our students also range widely. Some students come to us well prepared and excel, while others find the transition to a university academically challenging and benefit from intensive advising and academic support programs. This diversity in our student body meant that we needed to take into consideration the variety of different learning styles that our students employ.

Given this diversity, a common dialogue was needed to establish and maintain connections across the many subcultures within the larger university community. Accordingly, we undertook an extensive effort to engage in discussions with the colleges and schools, faculty, staff, administrators, students, alumni, and employers to understand what a meaningful learning experience meant to them and what their desired educational outcomes were.

Initially, this dialogue seemed like a cacophony of voices, but in listening to the various constituencies we found a confluence of conversations— a set of common themes. By engaging all of our constituencies in this dialogue, our focus emerged organically from those who had a vested interest in the outcome of the process, in particular the faculty. Initial focus group discussions with faculty identified the value of applied learning in fostering critical thinking outcomes for our students. These ideas were refined over time through further campus dialogue to reflect the ultimate focus of our plan: We wanted our students to have an educational experience characterized by active learning and to learn the higher-order thinking skills of application, analysis, synthesis, and evaluation.

This extended dialogue also meant that our constituencies drove the process in finding these answers. It took into account their respective subcultures and concerns and also enabled each member of the university community to feel a sense of ownership in the plans for enhancing student learning. As a result, the various constituencies in the university community were more willing to embrace the pedagogical change we were seeking, thus facilitating its institutionalization throughout the campus.

Model of Institutionalization. University leaders cannot simply plan for the sake of planning; they must plan to implement. No matter how good the ideas for pedagogical change are, they must be implemented in a way that enables faculty members to incorporate the desired approaches and learning outcomes in their classes, generates momentum for the institutionalization of the ideas, and allows for adaptation and the development of best practices. Our planning for implementation was guided by a set of four recommendations, developed in a Faculty Senate focus group meeting, for turning our theme of active learning into a viable plan to enhance student learning: (1) allow for innovation across schools and colleges; (2) begin with a focus on the undergraduate experience; (3) identify models of active learning experiences and the student learning outcomes that can be derived from them through an RFP process; and (4) develop a plan that focuses on these models and demonstrates how they might serve as the basis for expanding active learning initiatives across campus.

These recommendations also helped integrate our campus culture as well as facilitate implementation of our plans to enhance our students' educational experience. Allowing innovation to arise from the various academic units recognized our strong college model and that faculty members were in the best position to create new and exciting ways to implement active learning techniques in the classroom. The focus on undergraduate education would assist the university in ascertaining what teaching techniques worked best with the learning styles of our diverse and changing student body. Implicit in the third and fourth recommendations was the desire to learn from those faculty members already using or willing to use active learning techniques to help spread teaching excellence throughout the campus. Further, this approach would allow us to use our scholarship to inform our teaching, thus remaining sensitive to the university's dual culture. Putting these recommendations into practice resulted in the use of pilot projects (discussed below) that would enable the university to learn more about the institution as well as effective teaching and pedagogy.

Another important component in planning to implement is to make appropriate tools and resources available to faculty so that they have the skills and support necessary to bring about institution-wide pedagogical change. At UT Arlington, we put on numerous programs, seminars, and workshops with nationally recognized experts on topics such as developing and assessing student learning outcomes, developing active learning course experiences, and assessment and utilization of rubrics. Other implementation tools include instructional support sessions, communities of practice, teaching circles, orientation and mentoring programs for new faculty, continued recognition of teaching excellence through awards, and support grants and stipends for designated activities. Many of these tools do not require significant funding, yet they are useful in promoting a culture of furthering teaching excellence informed by our own research on the use of effective pedagogy.

Intentionality of Design. At UT Arlington, we approached our plan to enhance student learning from an institutional research perspective, which required an intentional and well thought-out research design. We created a narrowly tailored institutional research project, together with research questions and hypotheses, to study the acquisition and development of higher-order thinking skills in our students and to determine how active learning and its attendant effects can best be accomplished in the classroom. We also developed assessment strategies at the course, program, and university levels to evaluate the intervention of active learning techniques.

NEW DIRECTIONS FOR TEACHING AND LEARNING • DOI: 10.1002/tl

At the heart of our institutional study were twelve intentionally designed experiential courses employing active learning techniques. These pilot projects were selected based on certain commonalities (similar approaches and concepts and most importantly similar student learning outcomes), and covered nearly all the colleges and schools in the university, a broad range of the undergraduate experiences from introductory classes to capstone courses, and a wide variety of learning environments. The pilot project approach enabled us to begin by showcasing the work of committed, enthusiastic proponents of our goals. Over time, the visibility of these successful projects created interest among additional faculty who joined the effort to bring about pedagogical change.

One significant challenge in implementing this research design was developing the appropriate course-level assessments for each class. On one hand, to make the data derived from the pilot projects meaningful for comparative purposes, each course needed to utilize common assessment techniques. On the other hand, the importance given to allowing the pilot project instructors to drive the process meant that the assessment tools needed to work within each individual class. To balance these needs, we employed a common set of assessment tools that would be used in each pilot project course, such as the IDEA Student Rating of Instruction Tool, modified knowledge surveys (Nuhfer and Knipp, 2003), formative and summative assessments, the Active Learning Inventory Tool (Van Amburgh and others, 2007), and a course reflection memo. Working with the course instructors, however, we let them determine the specific manner in which these common tools would be used within their course. This way, assessing the intervention of active learning techniques would be a natural part of the class, making the data more meaningful and useful for future planning purposes.

Lessons Learned from the UT Arlington Process

Although we culled many lessons from our process of trying to develop an institutional commitment to experiential learning, two stand out for achieving success. First, the development and implementation of the plan for change needs to be natural, flow from the culture and goals of the institution, and fit within the experiences of each course. Second, the faculty must be a central part in developing and implementing the plan, and should be given the flexibility and encouragement to innovate.

Attention needs to be paid to the course-level implementation of any plan to institutionalize pedagogical change, for our experience at UT Arlington has shown that this is where the plan will succeed or fail. This means that the instructor needs to determine which experiential education intervention would integrate with and build upon the natural experiences of the course. Also, assessment needs to fit naturally within the course, and the instructor should be allowed to direct the process. Unless the intervention and assessment fit naturally within the course, they may disrupt the class as an artificial overlay—in other words, the students may feel that they are doing a task simply for the sake of doing it rather than actually learning from it.

Incorporating experiential education into the classroom requires a commitment from the faculty. Although many faculty members at our campus were using active learning and experiential education techniques, fitting these techniques into a larger institutional research project proved to be challenging. We incurred attrition as some of the pilot projects withdrew from our research project because the level and type of assessment needed for evaluating the university's plan as a whole did not fit as well with the course content as initially anticipated.

This point emphasizes the need for an institutional commitment to encourage faculty to innovate and adapt. In some cases where implementation problems initially arose, we were able to work through the issues with the faculty members by modifying the assessment tools to be used within their classes. In other cases, a faculty member would modify the manner in which the active learning/experiential education intervention was to be utilized. Working through these implementation issues may be difficult, but doing so helps build a set of best practices and experiences from which the university as a whole can learn. In this regard, the institution can become a learning organization itself, and use the evidence of teaching and student learning accomplishments derived from faculty experiences to better enable the university to develop teaching goals and strategies to reach its institutional objectives.

References

Nuhfer, E. and Knipp, D. "The Knowledge Survey: A Tool for All Reasons." In C. Wehlburg and S. Blossey (eds.), *To Improve the Academy: Resources for Faculty, Instructional, and Organizational Development*, vol. 21. Bolton, MA: Anker Publishing Company, 2003.

University of Texas at Arlington. Quality Enhancement Plan, 2007. Retrieved November 19, 2009, from http://activelearning.uta.edu/qep/assets/FinalQEP.pdf.

Van Amburgh, J. A., Devlin, J. W., Kirwin, J. L., and Qualters, D. M. "A Tool for Measuring Active Learning in the Classroom." *American Journal of Pharmaceutical Education*, 71(5), Article 85, 2007. Retrieved March 12, 2010, from http://www.ncbi.nlm.nih.gov/pmc/articles/PMC2064883/.

VICTORIA FARRAR-MYERS *is a professor of political science at the University of Texas at Arlington and was the university coordinator of its Quality Enhancement Plan for the school's reaffirmation process.*

DANA DUNN *is an associate professor of sociology at the University of Texas at Arlington and former provost responsible for the development of the Quality Enhancement Plan.*

Part B: The Odyssey Program at Hendrix College

Nancy P. Fleming, Mark S. Schantz

Like many similar institutions, Hendrix, a liberal arts college of approximately 1,400 students located in Conway, Arkansas, experienced declining enrollments and decreased revenues as a result of the recession of 2001–2003. At the opening faculty meeting of the 2003 fall semester, J. Timothy Cloyd, President of the College, called on us to be bold in our response to the challenges created by the economic downturn: "Instead of thinking in terms of how we can do things a little bit better each year, we must think in terms of how we should respond to reposition Hendrix in the face of a radically different and challenging external environment" (August 2003). Two years later, "Your Hendrix Odyssey: Engaging in Active Learning," an engaged learning program, was up and running. Since that time, enrollment at the college has grown dramatically and the institution has been able to significantly raise tuition, thus increasing net revenue. Now Odyssey is firmly entrenched as a graduation requirement and a defining element of campus culture.

Development of the Odyssey Program

Market research by a higher education consulting firm suggested that descriptions of Hendrix as a "demanding yet supportive" campus where hands-on learning was highly valued had particular resonance with pools of interested inquirers and applicants. A series of campus forums confirmed that this image appealed at home as well. Armed with this information and backed by the full support of the Board of Trustees, who pledged to raise the money necessary to make the vision real, the President commissioned a task force of faculty and students to develop the "Galileo Project," as the Odyssey Program was first named. In particular, the group was asked to consider what sorts of experiences could legitimately qualify as "hands-on" learning, and how much of this activity was already occurring on campus. In addition, they were charged with determining what other opportunities would need to be created "in order for Hendrix to claim, confidently and legitimately, that we provide for every student a 'hands-on' liberal arts education in a demanding yet supportive environment" (Cloyd, unpublished memo, 2003). By the end of the 2004 spring semester, the "Galileo Project" had been renamed "Odyssey," and its essential outlines had been approved by a faculty vote.

NEW DIRECTIONS FOR TEACHING AND LEARNING, no. 124, Winter 2010 © Wiley Periodicals, Inc.
Published online in Wiley Online Library (wileyonlinelibrary.com) • DOI: 10.1002/tl.424

The Odyssey Program was formally launched on Founders Day, October 26, 2004. Working quickly, the task force labored throughout the 2004–2005 academic year to craft the structure and content of the program. In the fall of 2005, the first group of students subject to the Odyssey requirement matriculated at the college.

Distinctive Features of the Program

The Odyssey Program drew heavily on activities already in place while also allowing for new opportunities for students and faculty. It has a number of distinctive features which have drawn national attention to the college.

The program is extraordinarily broadbased and includes six categories of engaged learning: Artistic Creativity (AC), Global Awareness (GA), Professional and Leadership Development (PL), Service to the World (SW), Undergraduate Research (UR), and Special Projects (SP). Combined, these categories cover most forms of experiential learning typically found on college campuses, such as internships, study abroad, volunteer work, community engagement, undergraduate research, and artistic activities. In addition, the sixth category, SP, makes room for interdisciplinary, nontraditional, unusual, or less easily classified ways of learning.

To graduate from Hendrix, all students must complete a minimum of three Odyssey projects, each one representing a different category. This requirement ensures that every student samples a variety of engaged learning activities and thereby cultivates the kind of breadth that lies at the heart of the liberal arts experience. Each student accumulates Odyssey credits on a special transcript that includes brief descriptions of his or her completed projects. This transcript is available to the student on request, in the same manner as the academic transcript, and can be used to supplement graduate school and job applications.

The program is flexible and can be tailored to each student's particular needs and strengths. Students may choose to fulfill the Odyssey requirement by participating in classes and co-curricular activities that have been preapproved for credit, or they may opt to design and propose their own projects. Funding is available on a competitive basis to help underwrite the expenses of individually designed projects. Regardless of which option the student chooses, the student must enlist the support and guidance of an appropriate faculty or administrative sponsor.

Finally, students are encouraged to do more than simply participate in an activity. In several categories (GA, PL, SW, and SP), students are required to work with their supervisors to reflect orally or in writing about the meaning of the experience and the learning that has taken place. For AC projects, the activity culminates in an artistic product—a performance, exhibit, or manuscript. Students who do research for a UR credit must present their results publicly. Thus, in each instance, the student must synthesize the experience and think carefully about its value and its consequences.

The Evolution of Odyssey

By most obvious measures, the Odyssey Program is highly successful both on campus and off. Of the first class subject to the requirement, fully ninety percent completed it in time to receive their diplomas at graduation in May 2009, an admirable record for a new program. Odyssey has also brought the college heightened national attention, and enrollment has grown substantially: in 2005, the entering class of freshmen and transfer students numbered 295, while in 2008, there were 451. Over the same time period, the college increased its tuition by more than forty percent. To help partially offset the higher cost, many incoming students are given "Odyssey Awards" as part of their financial aid packages. These scholarships are designed to recognize achievement in one of the Odyssey categories at the high school level, thus affirming the value of engaged learning early in a student's academic career.

Less quantifiable, but still palpable, is the manner in which the language and philosophy of Odyssey have become an integral part of the Hendrix experience. Even alumni who did not participate in the program as undergraduates have begun to speak of their "Hendrix Odysseys." Each year, six alumni are awarded Odyssey Medals for their outstanding achievements, one in each of the categories. The medals are presented in a formal ceremony on campus, a gesture that publicly recognizes and celebrates the love of lifelong learning that Hendrix hopes to foster in its students.

Thus, in six short years the Odyssey Program has developed from the glimmer of an idea suggested by market research to a fully fledged and burgeoning program that has brought national recognition to the college and has permeated the life and language of Hendrix to an unanticipated extent. What are the reasons for such speedy and widespread assimilation and success? The factors that have contributed to that success include the high level of engaged learning that was already taking place on campus, the range of categories, the flexibility of options and funding opportunities for students, the involvement of all members of the community (including trustees), and the availability of graduation credit. The success of the Odyssey Program, while presenting new challenges, has beneficially transformed Hendrix College.

Extension of Existing Activities. The Odyssey Program was built on elements of the campus culture that were already present. Students had been heavily involved in many activities that are now recognized as Odyssey-worthy, such as research; theatrical productions and classes in studio art, applied music, drama, and dance; internships; study abroad; mission trips and service work; and leadership opportunities in student organizations. The

New Directions for Teaching and Learning • DOI: 10.1002/tl

program recognizes and validates these activities as genuine learning opportunities, and as a result, many of them have actually attracted more participation. For example, the number of internships in 2005–2006 was 43, while in 2008–2009 there were 78. Similarly, the number of students studying abroad, either through formal programs or on shorter trips for specific projects, has increased dramatically: from 81 in 2005 to 143 by 2008–2009.

Flexibility and Funding for Students. Odyssey gives students the opportunity to "dream big" and design projects that they might not otherwise have undertaken. This aspect of the program immediately captured the students' imaginations. During the first three years, even many of those students who were not required to participate were quick to take advantage of the opportunity to realize their dreams. Funding is available on a competitive basis for those who need it. By April 2009, the Committee on Engaged Learning, which evaluates student funding requests and awards Odyssey grants, had awarded almost 1.2 million dollars to fund 240 projects that collectively involved 687 students.

Those of us who work with the Odyssey Program are constantly amazed at the creativity and resourcefulness demonstrated by the proposals we read. There are far too many truly fine projects to enumerate here, but the following examples give some of the flavor. On campus, students have restored an antiquated ceramics kiln, designed a labyrinth, and filled several neglected aquariums with living salt-water coral reef ecosystems. One noteworthy project, recently in its third summer, works in collaboration with the local Boys and Girls Club to bring third- through eighth-graders to campus for two days, during which the children are led through hands-on chemistry and biology experiments, thus exposing them to the joys of scientific discovery. Further afield, students have filled medical internships in Mexico and Zanzibar; studied the culture of people living with AIDS in New York and San Francisco, and the manifestation of racial tension among fans attending the World Soccer Cup games in Germany and Spain; they have attended workshops in writing, ballet, epigraphy, and country fiddling; they have interned with lawyers, politicians, opticians, and pipe organ builders; they have spent time living in Buddhist monasteries in Japan and on organic farms in Tennessee and Ireland. The Odyssey Program has offered students the opportunity to follow their passions as well as explore new interests.

The Odyssey Office features presentations by many of the students in a series known as the Odyssey Exemplars. Through this mechanism students teach each other about the possibilities and excitement of engaged learning. As a consequence, proposals and funding requests have grown stronger over time. While raising the bar has increased the competition for funding it also has had the unforeseen consequence of forcing students to learn how to write better proposals, a skill that may prove very useful to them in their future careers.

Community Involvement. Odyssey is a community-wide endeavor. Faculty and administrative staff not only serve as mentors for student projects, but are encouraged to submit proposals of their own for projects that include either individual students or groups. The availability of funding has made possible faculty-designed projects as diverse as a study of literature and its relationship to the land in South Africa (UR), archaeological field work in New Mexico (PL), a summer enrichment program for at-risk third-graders in Forrest City, Arkansas (SW), and the preparation of an oral and photographic history of women in San Luís, Costa Rica (SP). In addition to these far-flung examples, faculty-sponsored projects also take place closer to home. In 2005 the Hendrix College Chamber Orchestra recorded a professional CD of music by Alan Hovhaness in the college chapel (AC), and members of the natural science faculty frequently involve students in their summer research for Odyssey credit.

Several endowed "Odyssey Professorships," which provide funds of up to $25,000 per year, are also available to faculty who wish to devote one to three years developing and implementing engaged learning opportunities for students. At the time of this writing, thanks to the leadership of the trustees, six such professorships have been fully funded and awarded. The faculty members who hold them come from a range of disciplines: chemistry, religion, politics, economics, biology, and education.

Academic Credit. The use of an Odyssey transcript underscores the importance of engaged learning at Hendrix. Anecdotal evidence suggests that parents of current and prospective students especially value a document that can provide evidence of enhanced educational activities to graduate school admissions committees and future employers. We look forward to hearing from the first group of Odyssey alumni regarding the usefulness of this transcript from their perspective.

Campus Transformation. While the program built on and codified many aspects of who we already were, there is no doubt that Odyssey has also transformed the campus. Not only are there more students, but more of them come from a further distance, bringing with them the perspectives of other places. In 2005–2006, 46.1 percent of Hendrix students were from out-of-state; in 2008–2009, 59.9 percent came from outside Arkansas. The increasing number of students participating in Odyssey adventures around the globe has further enriched the campus with a wider worldview.

In addition, many of the faculty have begun to look at pedagogy in different ways, exploring options for bringing more engagement into our classrooms and looking for ways to link Odyssey experiences to more traditional learning. We have discovered that while theory does indeed inform practice, the lessons learned through Odyssey activities can just as profoundly enhance discussions in the classroom.

The Future of Odyssey

With success there are always new challenges. As we look to the future, we must find ways to keep the Odyssey Program fresh and lively; already there is discussion of what "Odyssey 2.0" will look like. We must devise ways to assess what students are learning through their Odyssey experiences and build on what we discover. We must also keep alive the dialogue about the relationship between experiential and traditional learning pedagogies to make sure that the balance remains appropriate for Hendrix.

As we engage in these conversations, we may find ways to weave the Odyssey ethos even more snugly into both co-curricular and curricular programs. Some faculty members are already engaged in a project funded by the Mellon Foundation in which they will design clusters of three or four courses that share interdisciplinary threads. Students who participate in these clusters will receive two Odyssey credits: a UR credit for a research project that will serve as the capstone to the experience and an SP credit for completing the coursework and keeping a journal that reflects on the connections among the classes. Wherever this road may ultimately lead us, the first stage of the Odyssey Program has opened exciting new worlds to students and faculty alike at Hendrix College.

References

Cloyd, J. T. Unpublished memo: charge to the Galileo Task Force. November 17, 2003.
Cloyd, J. T. Unpublished speech to the Hendrix College faculty. Conway, AR. August 19, 2003.

NANCY P. FLEMING is the director of the Odyssey Program and a professor of music at Hendrix College.

MARK S. SCHANTZ is the former director of the Odyssey Program and a professor of history at Hendrix College. Currently he is provost at Birmingham-Southern College.

Part C: Putting Experiential Education into Practice: Using Kolb as a Learning Model for Implementing Organizational Change

James R. Johnson, Ronald J. Kovach, Patricia N. Roberson

Purdue University Calumet (PUC), located in Hammond, Indiana, is the largest regional campus in the Purdue University system. It was founded in 1946, and its current enrollment is 10,100 graduate and undergraduate students. Headed by a Chancellor, the university is organized into six schools.

This chapter will discuss the use of David A. Kolb's Experiential Learning Model in the implementation of innovative graduation requirements in experiential education that began in 2008. Experiential Learning @ PUC (ExL) was designed to create distinction among other universities and develop a niche by improving the education of its students. As a result, a strategic initiative began in 2005. It was understood that the initiative would need to involve the entire campus community and faculty. This deliberate approach would require a carefully thought out organizational change process, as it would require a different way of teaching for many disciplines. The decision was made to use a metaimplementation model based on Kolb's theories, along with action learning. Our experience with this process provides the basis of this chapter. The decision led to success in its initial year (Table 9C.1).

Experiential Education Development

How did we accomplish this task? It was done through a metaimplementation of two theories: Kolb's theory of Experiential Learning (1984) and Action Learning Steps (Marquardt, 1996). By stringently applying the eight Standards of Practice of the National Society for Experiential Education, and by using the four stages of Kolb's cycle—Concrete Experience, Reflective Observation, Abstract Concept, and Active Experimentation—we were able to construct a plan of implementation.

Reflective Observation on the Implementation

An event in the implementation process illustrated the use of these theories. The ExL Task Force team that was formed early in the process became

NEW DIRECTIONS FOR TEACHING AND LEARNING, no. 124, Winter 2010 © Wiley Periodicals, Inc.
Published online in Wiley Online Library (wileyonlinelibrary.com) • DOI: 10.1002/tl.425

Table 9C.1. Status of Experiential Learning @ PUC in Year 1

Number of ExL courses developed	Number of ExL courses offered	Number of students enrolled in ExL courses
91	45	1,063

known as an *action learning set*. Marquardt (1996) defines an action learning set as "the core entity in group action learning group or team" (p. 41). This learning set was comprised of faculty members and administrators.

As the authors of this chapter engaged in "reflective observation" on the successful implementation of this initiative, we conclude that the implementation team members were what is widely known as "unconsciously competent." We realized that we had unconsciously used these two related theories as the framework for the experiential learning implementation. We took concrete experiences, reflected upon them, formed improved conceptualizations, and experimented by using the improved conceptualizations. Further, we realized that we had been engaging in action learning, in that real people were taking real action on real problems in real time and learning while doing so (Waddill and Marquardt, 2003, p. 407).

Throughout our process of implementation there was an overarching meta-cycle that will be illustrated in this case study. However, like any process, the reality is far more complicated than the developed model presented; within each stage were micro-Experiential Learning cycles that occurred. Additionally, the cycle does not occur only one time. As PUC progresses toward graduating their first class with this graduation requirement in place, the learning cycle keeps pace. The organization continues to change and adapt based on what we have experienced and what we have learned from past and current events.

The major thrust of the plan was to be transformative; that is, to move the institution into a position of uniqueness and to create a distinct "brand." It was decided early on that development efforts would bring about the anticipated transformation by developing the most valuable resource—faculty and staff—thus creating institutional expertise in experiential learning which would serve as the catalyst for organizational change. Most of the activities requiring funding were supported by a Department of Education Title III grant that began the transformation and that was expressly written for experiential learning faculty development initiatives (Purdue University Calumet, 2006).

The cycle of metaimplementation illustrated in Figure 9C.1 is the first of many cycles for this organization's learning process and is the basis for how we implemented an encompassing Experiential Learning program. Next, we will explain the core components to each stage and then illustrate the specific activities PUC implemented as it followed the metaimplementation cycle. Table 9C.2 summarizes these activities.

Figure 9C.1. Cycle of Metaimplementation

•Active Experimentation

•Concrete Experience

Closing the Gaps
and
Implementation of
Policy

Gathering
Information
and
Establishing Goals

Group
Brainstorming
and
Development of
Organization Policy

Sharing Information
Learned
and
Finding the Gaps

•Abstract Conceptualization

•Reflective Observation

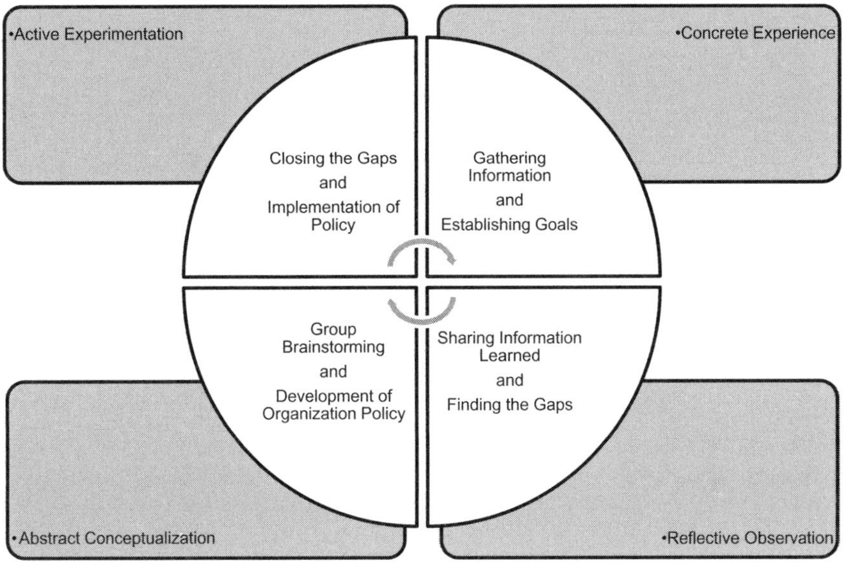

Source: Adapted from Kolb, 1984.

Table 9C.2. Key Activities During the Stages of Metaimplementation

Stage	*Key Activities*	
Concrete	***Gathering Information*** Joined NSEE. Established that PUC needed a program to make the learning environment richer. Established contacts at a similar school with experiential programs.	***Establishing Goals*** Formed an ad hoc committee to design an implementation plan. Wrote and received Department of Education Title III grant.
Active Reflection	***Sharing Information Learned*** Attended Martha's Vineyard Summer Institute on Experiential Learning for faculty and staff. Held university-wide informational sessions outlining the plans and explaining NSEE Standards of Practice on experiential learning	***Finding the Gaps*** Put forth resolution to Faculty Senate to establish an Experiential Learning task force subcommittee to study the issue. Implemented research study to establish a benchmark of

Table 9C.2. (*Continued*)

Stage	Key Activities	
	(academic department meetings, academic government body meetings, administrative governance groups, academic administrative group).	Experiential Learning courses at PUC. Conducted student survey to explore student body knowledge of Experiential Learning.
Abstract Conceptualization	**Brainstorming** Developed task force groups for each of the core areas needing improvement. Developed Experiential Learning types. Developed operationalization of NSEE standards.	**Development of Policy** Designed curriculum development and approval process specifically for experiential learning-designated courses by applying NSEE Standards of Practice. Developed Experiential Learning logo and advertisement plan. Planned for institutional changes (track and label courses, hire new staff to focus on Experiential Learning).
Active Experimentation	**Closing the Gaps** Developed task force groups for each of the core areas needing improvement. Conducted faculty development workshops. Established faculty development grants for creation (or revision) of courses with experiential learning components. Launched advertising campaign targeting students, community, and parents.	**Implementation of Policy** Put forth resolution to Faculty Senate for Experiential Learning graduation requirement. Created a permanent subcommittee of the Senate's Curriculum and Educational Policies Committee to approve the Experiential Learning designation. Passed first round of Experiential Learning courses that met NSEE standards.

Concrete Experience. *Concrete Experience* is the first stage in the metaimplementation process. When implementing a new program, concrete experience cannot be gained through happenstance; the organization must actively seek out the experience and label the experience by *Gathering Information* and *Goal Setting*. The organization must gather information about itself, the theories that are applicable, and practical examples that could be mimicked. This knowledge itself is not really an experience until it is labeled and worked into broad goals, such as "Our organization will implement an Experiential Learning course requirement," as PUC did. Once the goals are established, the base of the first experience is established and the organization can move toward building a framework, such as establishing funding or designating a leader.

Active Reflection. *Active Reflection* is the next stage in the Experiential Learning Cycle. An organization's reflection is often accomplished in a public forum, where as many people as possible can participate in the reflection. *Sharing Information Learned* from the Concrete Experience with the entire organization is how we actively reflected. Specifically, PUC chose to reflect in a public forum through presentations in the departments, at staff meetings, and to the faculty senate. Each time the information was shared with a new group or was repeated, the concept became clearer. Attendees from different areas of the organization reflected upon what the experience meant to them and their area. The ability to hear diverging points of view regarding the same subject enabled us to understand the theory and program better, because we were more aware of the different perceptions. The second component of Active Reflection in the metaimplementation process is *Finding the Gaps*. As the team actively reflected in a public forum, we also reflected on the new information gleaned and began to see patterns identifying where the most work needed to be done prior to implementation. The reflection process is always the appropriate time to list and define the gaps in the organization. For PUC, we learned that the gaps were centered in faculty development, course quantity, and organizational shared knowledge.

Abstract Conceptualization. The *Abstract Conceptualization* stage in organizational metaimplementation emphasizes application of the theories, goals, and information about your organization. The two key components include *Brainstorming Groups* and *Development of Policy*. The organization must develop a means by which representatives from all parts of the organization can effectively brainstorm and join theory and experience. We accomplished this by establishing taskforce groups that met once a month. These groups were the driving forces for development of policy. The policy and organization must reflect the gaps in the organization and must attempt to accomplish the overarching goals set forth in the concrete experience stage. Policy can also include delineation of how the organization chooses to define Experiential Learning and how a course is labeled as Experiential Learning. Our organization chose to define types of

Experiential Learning and incorporate the NSEE standards into our policy when labeling courses.

Active Experimentation. Finally, the time for *Active Experimentation* arrives, and the organization begins to implement the program. One key component of this stage is *Implementation of Policy*. Based on the theory learned, the knowledge gained from active reflection with the organization, and the policy the task forces developed, we were able to achieve the broad goal we set at the start: "Make Experiential Learning a graduation requirement." We accomplished this goal by enacting a policy in the Faculty Senate requiring Experiential Learning to be a graduation requirement. The second key component to this stage is the *Closing the Gaps* of the organization. In previous stages, the organization recognized the gaps that must be filled for successful implementation and identified how to fill them. During this stage, the organization must implement those programs in ways that close those gaps. In our organization, we focused on faculty development, increasing the organization's knowledge of the program (advertising), and increasing the number of courses accredited with Experiential Learning.

Implications for Future Research

While early in the process, several important issues have emerged at PUC. The first issue concerns the assessment of the experiential learning requirement and its effectiveness: Does it better prepare students? Does it increase student learning? Does it increase student retention? Does it improve time to graduate? The second issue dealt with how the experiential learning designator should be monitored: Will course changes over time dilute the content, thereby no longer allowing them to meet the eight standards? Will instructor turnover impact the experiential learning course content? Is there a need to evaluate course effectiveness differently than other courses? The last issue was whether the organizational change model utilized at PUC—that is, Kolb as an action learning model—was generalizable to other institutions.

Mezirow (1991, p. 189) suggests that "Transformation in the way one lives and thinks therefore becomes the ultimate criterion for evaluating adult education." This begs the question: How does PUC measure the manner in which one lives and thinks?

In conclusion, we have presented a method by which the desired learning outcomes for establishing experiential learning courses as a graduation requirement were actually practiced and demonstrated using Kolb's Experiential Learning Cycle and action learning steps as an organizational change methodology. This led us, as both faculty and administrators, to directly practice experiential learning steps while helping transform Purdue Calumet into an experiential learning university, thereby demonstrating to the campus and to students the very best elements of adult experiential learning.

NEW DIRECTIONS FOR TEACHING AND LEARNING • DOI: 10.1002/tl

References

Kolb, D. A. *Experiential Learning: Experience as the Source of Learning and Development.* Englewood Cliffs, NJ: Prentice-Hall, 1984.

Livingston, J. S. "Myth of the Well-Educated Manager." In Harvard Business Review (ed.), *Business Classics: Fifteen Key Concepts for Managerial Success.* Boston: Harvard Business School Publishing, 1971.

Marquardt, M. *Building the Learning Organization.* New York: McGraw-Hill, 1996.

Mezirow, J. *Transformative Dimensions of Adult Learning.* San Francisco: Jossey-Bass Publishers, 1991.

Purdue University Calumet. 2006. "News Release: $1.7 Million Grant Received to Advance Experiential Education." Retrieved March 12, 2010, from http://www.calumet.purdue.edu/news/releases/06-12-07_exp-grant.html.

Waddill, D. D. and Marquardt, M. "Adult Learning Orientations and Action Learning." *Human Resource Development Review* 4, 2003, 406–429.

JAMES R. JOHNSON *is an associate professor in organizational leadership and supervision at Purdue University Calumet.*

RONALD J. KOVACH *is an assistant vice chancellor at Purdue University Calumet.*

PATRICIA N. ROBERSON *is a marriage and family therapist in Florida.*

NEW DIRECTIONS FOR TEACHING AND LEARNING • DOI: 10.1002/tl

10

Developing experiential education programs can be both rewarding and daunting. This chapter offers possible strategies for designing and implementing such programs.

Experiencing Success: Some Strategies for Planning the Program

Timothy Donovan, Richard Porter, James Stellar

The concept of experiential learning, in one form or another, has been around a long time, some would say going back to Confucius. More recently, however, within the United States it was put into practice in a very aggressive form, cooperative education, created by Herman Schneider and initiated at the University of Cincinnati (UC) in 1906. Shortly thereafter, in 1909, Northeastern University started its own version. As with Schneider's UC program, Northeastern's alternated periods of full-time work and periods of study. Interest in experiential education picked up again when significant federal funding became available in 1965, and it has recently gained ground globally as "work-integrated learning." In fact, with the expansion of internships, study abroad, service-learning, and undergraduate research, everyone nowadays seems to be interested in experiential education. Yet the best way for an institution to move forward in the creation or evolution of such a program is not always so clear, nor is it easy to discern the extent of the commitment needed.

Reflecting on Our Experiences

The present chapter grew out of a need of our own for a little clarity. Some years ago, as academic administrators at Northeastern, we wanted to more fully understand our signature educational enterprise of cooperative education, or "co-op." In particular, we needed to explore the question of what students actually learned (not just earned) while on the job, as well as how,

NEW DIRECTIONS FOR TEACHING AND LEARNING, no. 124, Winter 2010 © Wiley Periodicals, Inc.
Published online in Wiley Online Library (wileyonlinelibrary.com) • DOI: 10.1002/tl.426

or even whether, they were transferring their learning across the boundary that they, and even the faculty, often mark between time spent in the classroom and time spent outside of it.

These were particularly intriguing questions to us, since our own intellectual home was the College of Arts and Sciences, where the connections to learning from experience had most often been considered remote, at best. In addition, while these matters are important for new or existing programs to ponder, they were all the more pressing for us because we had already embarked on the adventure of making experiential education, broadly delineated, an academic requirement for graduation in the College.

After numerous meetings and seminars, and through various projects and centers dedicated to these issues, we were able to set a direction for delivering a rather comprehensive program well in time for our students to fulfill the requirement. Simultaneously, we had organized annual workshops for the faculty and professional staff during the summer at Martha's Vineyard, the island off the coast of Cape Cod renowned for its resident authors and artists. There we were teaching ourselves about the energy and expertise that had gone into various initiatives at Northeastern, while also learning where we still needed to go in enhancing our overall experiential effort. We also started thinking in terms of other schools we might attract to a special session that would be national and even international in reach. Joined by some distinguished guest speakers, we announced that applications were available for a new Summer Institute on Experiential Education at Martha's Vineyard.

We had responses from a number of universities and eventually hosted representatives of nearly forty schools over the first years of operation. They typically arrived in teams of three or more academic officers, faculty members, and other professionals in experiential education, ranging from professors and directors to deans and provosts. Each team focused on the main task of drafting a specific plan of action for its own campus. The discussions among the groups were usually informative and often inspiring, pointing the way toward ever-greater curricular innovation and resourceful administration. (The institute has since operated under the aegis of the World Association for Cooperative Education and has appropriately broadened its focus to include globalization of all experiential education.)

Based on our interactions with these and other colleagues over the years, at Northeastern as well as at the summer institutes, we have managed to formulate a few strategies to be considered in program planning. Some of these are perhaps a bit well-worn now, but they were certainly hard-earned, and derived mainly by reflecting on our own (mostly) successful experiential learning.

Strategies for Experiential Education Programs

Our first suggestion is to define "experiential" for the campus in terms of the institution as a whole. As we know, the dominant traditions within the academy tend not be in the realm of experiential education, although there might be several pockets of it on any campus. Some of these may not be readily identified as such, nor located under one roof (or Web site). However organized, programs in any case usually need some definition or philosophy that reflects the aims of their leadership and, importantly, those of the institution as a whole. The latter could perhaps be determined from published mission statements, where one may find, for example, that the university is committed to serving the greater community, given that maintaining good relations and citizenship is always a concern. This, then, could be an opportune place to begin discussing experiential education, especially service-learning and its obvious benefit to the community.

Another place from which to draw a definition of "experiential" might be the major self-studies that are regularly undertaken by institutions of higher learning, such as strategic planning or accreditation. Participation in these exercises can provide a special opportunity to talk to administrators, faculty, and staff about shaping initiatives that are compatible with the goals of the institution as a whole.

Yet another option might be to build upon an existing program, one that may already be well-established and understood—as was, for example, Cooperative Education at Northeastern. Whatever steps are taken, they are important in the process of setting up a continuum of information about the program that will be necessary in the long run. Eventually this message will find its way into everything from college brochures to final transcripts, not to mention the steady stream of publicity in alumni magazines and news releases that help "brand" the institution, including its (by then) ongoing commitment to experiential education.

Role of the Faculty. Our next suggestion is to fully engage the faculty in the planning and oversight of experiential curriculum. The faculty usually own the curriculum—and rightly so. As educators, they are the experts hired to take responsibility for what is taught and learned on campus. Therefore, it is both reasonable and desirable that they be involved as much as possible in the advancement of experiential education. Any relevant committee should include key faculty members from the academic areas most affected, and involvement by the department chairs should especially be sought. While some level of resistance to proposals might be encountered, just a few allies can often make the difference, and good ideas will usually prevail in the end. If barriers still remain, then the focus might be shifted from teaching methods to student outcomes, which can then be viewed advantageously through the lens of the learning desired, as opposed to pedagogical preferences or biases. This focus on outcomes leads to our next strategy.

Learning Goals. We believe it is useful, early on, to develop some general learning goals in the program, for, as the social psychologist Kurt Lewin (1951) has famously made known, there is nothing so practical as a good theory. A basic theory of learning or a set of goals can help structure the program, giving it a broad framework for the many kinds of learning to be achieved while also conveying, as may be necessary, a seriousness about the contribution being made to the academy. The set of goals that we originally developed in Arts and Sciences included *critical thinking* and *communications skills* as part of a student's intellectual growth; *field knowledge* and *technical skills* in academic growth; and *ethical/social awareness* and *career* and *individual development* as part of personal/professional growth. While no single course or activity could likely fulfill them all, and they are by no means the only goals possible, they served us rather well for a time, because they held in common many features of both a liberal arts philosophy and the diverse forms of experiential education. The goals can be readily interpreted (for example, using modern instrumentation, analytical techniques, data collection, computer applications) and prioritized differently by each academic discipline involved.

Quality Control. We recommend expanding the curriculum while monitoring for quality and student outcomes. Real standards must be set for any experiential course work, including the assigned readings, papers, hours, and credits. One way to ensure that significant learning, and not just an interesting experience, occurs is to establish an ad hoc committee. Each associated academic department should also be encouraged to take the initiative in proposing a curriculum attuned to its own discipline. Courses should be reviewed so that there is an expectation of excellence in the program itself as well as in outcomes to be achieved. Noncredit experiences could be subject to a similar analysis, since these can result in students becoming more passionately committed to their disciplines, thereby complementing academic learning and enriching subsequent classes.

Communities of Practice. While the phrase "community of practice" (Wenger, McDermott, and Snyder, 2002) might aptly describe the setting that students will ideally encounter in their work or service, it could also well describe the groups formed by experiential practitioners and supporters back on campus. Programs should cultivate both of these sorts of communities; the latter may be especially encouraged through faculty and staff development initiatives. Providing grants remains the tried-and-true way of nurturing development, as funding not only indicates intellectual respect but also purchases time in a busy schedule to focus on the design of new courses, classes, and activities. Communities may well develop naturally out of this pool as special interest groups and learning networks, or eventually become more formalized as, say, Faculty Fellows or Learning Circles. By sponsoring these communities, the institution encourages the production of a variety of best practices, such as ideas for class discussion, paper assignments, reflection, posters, journals, portfolios, and mentoring. Further, communities are comprised of a core of dedicated members who will, in turn, recruit others, thus serving to sustain things over time. Since such groups will typically circulate research published by the larger community in the profession itself, their cultivation by the institution may encourage publications (always prized) from among the members.

NEW DIRECTIONS FOR TEACHING AND LEARNING • DOI: 10.1002/tl

"Inside/Outside" Expertise. While it is important for organizations to look inward for answers, a good way to generate excitement and momentum for an experiential education program is to bring in outside speakers, carefully selected for the intended audience, and consultants with a carefully planned agenda so that information flows in all the right directions. The reverse of bringing the outside in, so to speak, is for colleagues to go *out* to regional and national conferences (with funding to do so) or to other notable institutions in order to benchmark progress back inside their home program. Another "outside" initiative that is unusually valuable is for faculty members to meet with the students and their supervisors on site. This is important for encouraging both student and supervisor, but also for the opportunity to give faculty more insight into the learning being achieved in that setting, whether it be a company, museum, statehouse, or even another country.

Student Showcases. Students are the principal clientele of any educational program, and yet student advisory groups are often overlooked or underutilized. Not only does it cost very little administrative energy to get them up and running, but such groups serve as a source of opinion on how well things are working and can provide testimonials which, coming from peers who have "been there," will seem more credible to other students. While success stories are, of course, frequently employed, they are often not sufficiently placed in the media that students view most often (YouTube, Facebook, and the like). This approach is particularly powerful when those media are interactive and not just a static projection of the institution on a brochure or a Web site. But all visitors to the various media should expect to see student profiles there as a matter of course.

Another opportunity for showcasing students is at an awards ceremony focused on the best achievements of the year. An annual expo can be an even better chance for displaying student accomplishments while also encouraging discussion about best practices by faculty, staff, and special guests such as university officials or potential donors. Of course, we all look to make contact with students where they are, and blogs not only can do that but also encourage more student writing and reflection, which any university should welcome.

Student Partnership and Growth. It is well demonstrated, especially at open houses or panel sessions, that students are good ambassadors for any program in which they have successfully participated. To stop there, however, would be to miss an opportunity for administrators to both get some help in running the program and to offer students a chance for further growth in different contexts. In the classroom context, for instance, undergraduates can often work in advising and tutoring centers; when enlisted as assistants in a specific course, they can be helpful with assignments and facilitation during conference hours or recitations. In the workplace context, students may participate in the hiring process of the next cohort. For example, co-op or internship students may be asked to sort through resumes and to advise on those which look promising during the selection of their potential successors. Students may participate in the resulting interviews as well as show newcomers around the company. In the context of the larger program, they can help identify appropriate placements, conduct mock interviews, lead reflection sessions, or edit blogs. Again, the aim is to keep providing timely experiences as opportunities for potential growth by students.

Conclusion

The renewed emphasis on experiential education may be a blessing for some schools—a chance to improve on recruitment and retention of students or perhaps to update and reinvigorate the curriculum. Yes, experiential education also has its pitfalls, certainly, since it typically involves faculty, staff, students, and supervisors all working in concert. By our count, that is at least two more variables than are usually involved in regular instruction (the teacher teaches, the students study), and thus more that could go wrong, possibly at some considerable expense. So we know that there are real and even daunting challenges here, as there always are in creating significant change on any campus.

Responsibility for determining the right strategies and implementing effective plans is usually up to a central academic office (provost, dean) in coordination with program offices (study abroad, co-op, and so on) and academic departments, backed by senior administrators. No single administrative model or flow chart ensures success, however, and you sometimes just have to take good leadership wherever you can find it and let it be exercised as well as can be at any and every level. The challenges are always well worth taking on and, with some planning and purpose, overcoming, because the rewards are so great for all concerned.

References

Lewin, K. *Field Theory in Social Science: Selected Theoretical Papers*. D. Cartwright, ed. New York: Harper & Row, 1951.

Wenger, E., McDermott, R., and Snyder, W. M. *Cultivating Communities of Practice: A Guide to Managing Knowledge*. Cambridge, MA: Harvard Business Press, 2002.

TIMOTHY DONOVAN *is a former chair of English and associate dean in arts and sciences at Northeastern University.*

RICHARD PORTER *is chair of mathematics and former vice president for cooperative education at Northeastern.*

JAMES STELLAR *is provost at Queens College, CUNY, and former dean of arts and sciences at Northeastern.*

11

Reflection is the key to making the most of experiential learning. Only by seriously addressing reflection as a curriculum strand can we insure that students really do integrate and transform their experiences into meaningful learning.

Making the Most of Learning Outside the Classroom

Donna M. Qualters

As you have seen in *Experiential Education: Making the Most of Learning Outside the Classroom*, experiential education is a powerful learning experience for students. But what is also clear is that experiential education can be a powerful experience for faculty, staff, administrators and the community as well. In other words, a well-thought-out, carefully conceived program of engaging students beyond the classroom walls enriches the university environment and the community in which it is located.

In many ways experiential education is truly authentic education, as it assists students in translating classroom knowledge into meaningful learning for their future. But what our authors make clear is that experiential education needs to be viewed as a unique form of pedagogy involving deep reflection, collaboration, and assessment. Unless experiences outside the classroom are brought into the classroom and integrated with the goals and objectives of the discipline theory, students will continue to have amazing outside experiences but will not readily connect them to their in-class learning. Without reflective experiential education programs, we educators lose a valuable opportunity to transform classroom and community learning into a deeper understanding of the world.

In his book *Why Don't Students Like School,* Daniel Willingham (2009) makes it clear that wherever we focus students' attention is what they will learn. Thus, in experiential education it is even more important to apply this principle as students digest, synthesize, and transform learning from multiple sources. The way to do so is through the practice of reflection.

NEW DIRECTIONS FOR TEACHING AND LEARNING, no. 124, Winter 2010 © Wiley Periodicals, Inc.
Published online in Wiley Online Library (wileyonlinelibrary.com) • DOI: 10.1002/tl.427

Without mastering the skill of deep reflection, students will learn much out in the world, but we, their faculty, will not really know whether they have learned what they needed to from the experience. More importantly, we will also not know what other connections they might have made as they apply what we have taught them in class to their experiences. Thinking back to David Thornton Moore's examples in Chapter 1, it is clear that students will need instruction in reflection just as in any other discipline skill if we are to provide them with more than just the experience. Many writers have talked about reflection and reflective practice, but we are advocating for much more: Without a careful curriculum involving structured, reflective skill building, students may never learn what we hope they will outside the four walls of the classroom.

Reflective Curriculum

So what would a reflective curriculum look like? Let me offer a couple of ideas. Joseph A. Raelin, in discussing work-based learning in Chapter 5, describes the stages and questions that students can pursue in order to reflect deeply. These can be one basis of establishing a strand within a curriculum. Another possibility, outlined by Graham Gibbs (1988) with his reflective cycle, can be the starting point for thinking about how to design a reflective curriculum for students.

This cycle begins with asking "What happened?" Students want to tell us their stories; they *need* to tell us their stories. Any significant reflection is going to begin at this descriptive level. But part of such storytelling is addressing the affective component: What students were thinking and feeling during the experience is as important as the experience itself. Therefore, the first step in teaching reflection may be to help students identify their feelings in a situation and then explore with them how those feelings translated into action. In my student teaching seminar, novice students are often amazed that they share similar experiences but feel very differently about them. One student may be upset when classroom management does not work, another is frustrated, another is angry, another is frightened. Each of these emotions will lead to a different path of resolution. Therefore, understanding the emotional response to a situation is a critical first step in determining which path of action to follow.

The second step in the cycle is evaluation. This is where students decide what was good about the situation and what was bad. It involves understanding the effectiveness of the experience and thinking about the learner's response to it. In emotional situations, students often have to be carefully guided to seeing the good, to seeing that through mistakes and mishaps, real learning occurs. Conversely, they need to see that even in the best of situations, something can be improved, rethought, or augmented. This kind of reflection begins to instill the necessary habit of continually thinking deeply about practice.

NEW DIRECTIONS FOR TEACHING AND LEARNING • DOI: 10.1002/tl

The next step in the cycle is the most difficult for students to grasp and understand—analysis. This requires asking students what sense they can make about the experience, and involves them in reconsidering the tacit assumptions they bring to the situation. While delving into those assumptions is difficult, it is the crux of reflection: analysis transforms learning. For educators, setting the climate for students to really probe their belief system is fraught with challenges. As Perrin Cohen points out in his discussion of reflective ethical engagement in Chapter 6, students will not engage in deep reflection until they feel it is comfortable and above all safe to do so. However, even safety does not necessarily lead to surfacing beliefs. Continually asking students to ask themselves the important questions of reflection— "What did I believe would happen here?" "Why did I believe it?" "Is what I believe true?"—is among the most intense experiences students can have in their learning career, and without it, growth is much more happenstance than planned. I tell my students that making decisions and taking action without examining their underlying beliefs is like throwing darts at a dartboard blindfolded. In other words, understanding that something does not work and trying something else without the reflective step results in trial and error rather than carefully thought-out change based on theory and practice. This step takes time, practice, and constant reinforcement. Deep reflection is like developing critical thinking—everyone agrees students need to do it, yet no one really takes ownership of teaching students how to do it. As teachers, we evaluate both their critical and reflective skills while assuming that someone else along the way has taught them to our students. Reflection, like critical thinking, is a learned skill, difficult to do well, and so it needs to be taught with patience and understanding, with safety and structure.

Once students master analysis with some facility, they can move more smoothly through the reflective cycle. They can brainstorm alternatives and finally complete the cycle by developing an action plan. If these questions are part of a structured approach throughout experiential learning— before, during, and after each experience—we will have provided students with the tools to make the most of their current and future learning, both inside and outside the classroom. Reflection does not simply happen; it must be carefully taught.

A third model on which to base a reflective curriculum is the Pedagogical Thinking Scale (Sparks-Langer and Colton, 1990). This scale includes seven levels of reflection ranging from the basic level, which lacks descriptive language—a simple layperson description of an event—to a much more sophisticated deeper level, which uses discipline theory, context factors, and ethical, moral, and political issues in the decision-making process. Research by Toh Wah Seng (2004) has modified this to a six-point scale (Table 11.1). Either of these scales can be seen as structured mastery levels of reflection that can be measured through assessment of student work. A teacher training program provides an excellent context in which to illustrate the use of such a model.

Table 11.1. Six-Point Reflective Pedagogical Thinking Scale

Level	Description/Criteria
1	Nonjudgmental report/description of events/supervisor's comments
2	Judgmental report/description of events/problem/supervisor's comments/ personal suggestions for future action with no reasons or justification/ rationale given
3	Descriptions/explanations of events/problems/personal suggestions for future actions with traditional/personal preferences given as reason/ justification/rationale
4	Description/explanation with principle or theory given as reason/ justification/rationale
5	Description/explanation with principle/theory and consideration of contextual factors given as reason/justification/rationale
6	Description/explanation with consideration of ethical, moral, and political issues

Source: Adapted from Seng, 2004, pp. 6–7.

In introductory education courses, students would be introduced to a scale, cycle, or series of questions representing the different levels of reflection. Next, they would begin their field work and start to reflect using journals or blogs. Instead of just reading and grading these reflections, instructors could identify for students the level, cycle area, or questions they have addressed in their responses and encourage them to go deeper. If the same framework continues through the next two years of their preparation, the students will begin to engage in a more sophisticated level of reflection. By their capstone experience (in education this is student teaching), students would be expected to demonstrate a measureable level of sophistication in their concurrent reflections with the peer colleagues.

Conclusion

As authors, we hope we have demonstrated in a theoretical and practical manner how to bring the outside into the classroom and the classroom outside into the greater world in a way that enriches your lives as teachers and the lives of both your students and those with whom they work, on campus, in their communities, and finally in the larger world they will explore post-graduation.

We encourage you to work together with colleagues, site placements, and the community in general to determine the best form your reflection curriculum should take. Working together and having a common method of talking about theory and practice, of exploring the learning that takes place, and of helping students become more independent and authentic in understanding how theory and practice come together to create new ideas and ways of knowing will be the cornerstone of an experiential program that adds significant value to student learning.

References

Gibbs, G. *Learning By Doing: A Guide to Teaching and Learning Methods.* Oxford: Further Education Unit, Oxford Polytechnic, 1988.

Seng, T. W. "Measuring Practicum Student Teachers' Reflexivity: The Reflective Pedagogical Thinking Scale." 2004. Retrieved March 25, 2010, from http://www.eric .ed.gov/ERICDocs/data/ericdocs2sql/content_storage_01/0000019b/80/1b/c4/34.pdf. (ED 490 778)

Sparks-Langer, G. M., and Colton, A. B. "Synthesis of Research on Teachers' Reflective Thinking." *Journal of Teacher Education*, 1990, *41*(4), 37–44.

Willingham, D. *Why Don't Students Like School? A Cognitive Scientist Answers Questions About How the Mind Works and What It Means for the Classroom.* San Francisco: Jossey-Bass, 2009.

DONNA M. QUALTERS is the director of the Center for Teaching Excellence and an associate professor of education at Suffolk University.

ADDITIONAL RESOURCES

Books and Articles

Where appropriate, a unique accession number is assigned to each reference in the additional resource section. This number is also referred to as ERIC Document Number (ED Number) and ERIC Journal Number (EJ Number).

Berry, H. A., and Chisholm, L. A. "Service-Learning in Higher Education around the World: An Initial Look." New York: The International Partnership for Service-Learning, 1999. (ED 439 654)

Bringle, R. G., and Duffy, D. K. (eds.). *With Service in Mind: Concepts and Models for Service-Learning in Psychology.* AAHE's Series on Service-Learning in the Disciplines. Washington, DC: AAHE, 1998. (ED 449 739)

Bringle, R. G., and Hatcher, J. A. "A Service-Learning Curriculum for Faculty." *The Michigan Journal of Community Service-Learning,* 1995, 2(1), 112–122. (EJ 552 434)

Bringle, R. G., Hatcher, J. A., and Games, R. "Engaging and Supporting Faculty in Service Learning." *Journal of Public Service and Outreach,* 1997, 2(1), 43–51. (EJ 566 426)

Dewey, J. *Moral Principles in Education.* Carbondale, IL: Southern Illinois University Press, 1975.

Droge, D., and Murphy, B. O. (eds.). *Voices of Strong Democracy: Concepts and Models for Service-Learning in Communication Studies.* AAHE's Series on Service-Learning in the Disciplines. Washington, DC: AAHE, 1999. (ED 449 728)

Eyler, J., and Giles, D. E. *Where's the Learning in Service-Learning?* San Francisco: Jossey-Bass, 1999. (ED 430 433)

Fisher, B. M. *No Angel in the Classroom: Teaching through Feminist Discourse.* Lanham, MD: Rowman and Littlefield, 2001.

Garvin, D. A. *Learning in Action: A Guide to Putting the Learning Organization to Work.* Boston: Harvard Business Press, 2000.

Giles, D. E. "Understanding an Emerging Field of Scholarship: Toward a Research Agenda for Engaged, Public Scholarship." *Journal of Higher Education Outreach and Engagement,* 2008, 12(2), 97–108.

Green, M. F., Luu, D., and Burris, B. *Mapping Internationalization on U.S. Campuses: 2008 Edition.* Washington, DC: American Council on Education, 2008.

Harkavy, I., and Donovan, B. M. (eds.). *Connecting Past and Present: Concepts and Models for Service-Learning in History.* AAHE's Series on Service-Learning in the Disciplines. Washington, DC: AAHE, 2000. (ED 449 732)

Hart, J. *Smiling through the Cultural Catastrophe: Toward the Revival of Higher Education.* New Haven, CT: Yale University Press, 2001.

Hutchins, R. M. "The Higher Learning in America." *Journal of Higher Education,* 1999, 70(5), 524–532. (EJ 595 192)

Kendall, J. C., and others. *Strengthening Experiential Education within Your Institution.* Raleigh, NC: National Society for Internships and Experiential Education, 1986. (ED271 055)

Knowles, M. S. *The Modern Practice of Adult Education: From Pedagogy to Andragogy* (2nd ed). Englewood Cliffs, NJ: Prentice Hall, 1980.

Liang, J. *Hello Real World: A Student's Approach to Great Internships, Co-ops, and Entry-Level Positions.* Charleston, SC: BookSurge, 2005.

Lindeman, E. C. *The Meaning of Adult Education: A Classic North American Statement on Adult Education.* New York: New Republic, Inc., 1989 (reprinted from 1961 edition, originally published in 1926). (ED 365 849)

Lisman, C. D., and Harvey, I. E. (eds.). *Beyond the Tower: Concepts and Models for Service-Learning in Philosophy.* AAHE's Series on Service-Learning in the Disciplines. Washington, DC: AAHE, 2000. (ED 449 737)

Merriam S. B., and Cunningham P. M. (eds.). *Handbook of Adult and Continuing Education.* Jossey-Bass Higher Education Series. San Francisco: Jossey-Bass, 1989. (ED 359 411)

Murphy, D., Scammel, M., and Sclove, R. (eds.). *Doing Community-Based Research: A Reader.* Amherst, MA, and Knoxville, TN: The Loka Center in partnership with the Community Partnership Center, 1997.

Newman, J. H. *The Idea of a University.* New Haven, CT: Yale University Press, 1996 (originally published 1873).

Ostrow, J., Hesser, G., and Enos, S. (eds.). *Cultivating the Sociological Imagination: Concepts and Models for Service-Learning in Sociology.* AAHE's Series on Service-Learning in the Disciplines. Washington, DC: AAHE, 1999. (ED 449 740)

Resnick, L. B. "The 1987 Presidential Address: Learning in School and Out." *Educational Researcher,* 1987, 16(9), 13–20. (EJ 368 309)

Rudolph, F. *The American College and University: A History.* Athens, GA: University of Georgia Press, 1991 (originally published in 1962).

Shor, I. *Empowering Education: Critical Teaching for Social Change.* Chicago: University of Chicago Press, 1992. (ED 359 303)

Shrader, E., Saunders, M. A., Marullo, S., Benatti, S., and Weigert, K. M. "Institutionalizing Community-Based Learning and Research: The Case for External Networks." *The Michigan Journal of Community Service-Learning,* 2008, 14(2), 27–40. (EJ 831 369)

Sigmon, R. L. "Service to Learn, Learning to Serve, Linking Service with Learning." Washington, DC: Council for Independent College Reports, 1994.

Sigmon, R. L. "Service-learning: Three Principles." *Synergist, National Center for Service-Learning, ACTION,* 1979, 8(1), 9–11.

Sigmon, R. L., and Colleagues (eds.). *The Journey to Service-Learning: Experiences from Independent Liberal Arts Colleges and Universities.* Washington, DC: Council of Independent Colleges, 1996. (ED 403 825)

Simon, R. I., Dippo, D., and Schenke, A. *Learning Work: A Critical Pedagogy of Work Education.* Critical Studies in Education and Culture Series. New York: Bergin and Garvey, 1991. (ED 385 733)

Sullivan, W. M., and Rosin, M. S. *A New Agenda for Higher Education: Shaping a Life of the Mind for Practice.* San Francisco: Jossey-Bass, 2008.

Svinicki, M. D., and Menges, R. J. (eds.). *Honoring Exemplary Teaching.* New Directions for Teaching and Learning, no. 65. San Francisco: Jossey-Bass, 1996. (EJ 523 130)

Trigwell, K., and Prosser, M. "Changing Approaches to Teaching: A Relational Perspective." *Studies in Higher Education,* 1996, 21(3), 275–284. (EJ 537 765)

Trigwell, K., and Prosser, M. "Congruence between Intention and Strategy in University Science Teachers' Approaches to Teaching." *Higher Education,* 1996, 32(1), 77–87. (EJ 529 647)

Experiential Education Programs and Supporting Organizations

All online resources retrieved April 15, 2010.

Connecticut College (New London, CT), Student-Faculty Research. www.conncoll.edu/sciences/1832.htm

Hendrix College (Conway, AR), Odyssey Program. www.hendrix.edu/odyssey/odyssey
.aspx
LaGuardia Community College (Long Island City, NY), Cooperative Education.
www.lagcc.cuny.edu/COOPEDU/default.htm
Long Island University Brooklyn Campus (Brooklyn, NY), Global College (formerly
Friends World College). www.brooklyn.liu.edu/globalcollege
National Society for Experiential Education. www.nsee.org
Northeastern University (Boston, MA), Experiential Learning. www.northeastern.edu/
experiential-learning
Purdue University Calumet (Hammond, IN), ExL. http://webs.calumet.purdue.edu/exl
University of Texas at Arlington (Arlington, TX), Community Service Learning.
www.uta.edu/ccsl
WACE Institute on Global and Experiential Education. www.waceinc.org/institute/
index.htm
World Association for Cooperative Education. www.waceinc.org

INDEX

Abstract Conceptualization, 81, 85–86
Action learning set, 82–82
Action Learning Steps (Marquardt), 81, 86
Action research model, 15
Active experimentation, 81, 86
Active Learning Inventory Tool (Van Amburgh), 73
Active reflection, 85
Adaptive Character of Thought (ACT) Theory (Anderson), 40
American Council on Education Report (2008), 25–28
Americans with Disabilities Act, 24
Anderson, J. R., 40
Angelo, T. A., 60
Aristotle, 7, 42
Arkansas, 79
Assessment, experiential education, 55–61; four essential questions in, 57; learning portfolio for, 60–61; and measuring learning, 58–60
Association of American Colleges and Universities, 32
Association of International Educators (NAFSA), 23
Astin, A., 58

Bailey, T. R., 9
Bandura, A., 42
Banta, T. W., 57
Beard, C., 63
Benson, L., 15
Biaggio, M., 26
Bloom, A., 7, 9
Bloom's taxonomy, 60
Boren Scholarship (National Security Education Program), 25
Boston, Massachusetts, 51, 63
Boud, D., 10
Bowie, W. R., 20
Boyer, E. L., 34
Bringle, R. G., 16
Brockingtong, J. L., 23
Bruner, J. S., 8, 44
Buddhist monastaries (Japan), 78
Burkhardt, J. C., 7
Butin, D. W., 5, 7

Cape Cod, Massachusetts, 90
CBE. *See* Community-based research (CBE)
CBLR. *See* Community-based learning and research (CBLR)
Chaiklin, S., 4
Chambers, T. C., 7
Chapdelaine, A., 28
Cheek, T., 63
Chenevert, J., 31, 33
Chenoweth, M. S., 26
Cloyd, J. T., 75
Cohen, M. D., 40
Cohen, P., 47, 48, 51, 53, 97
Cohen, R., 10
Cole, J. B., 24
College Learning for the New Global Century (Association of American Colleges and Universities), 32
College: The Undergraduate Experience in America (Boyer), 34
Collier, P. J., 5, 15
Collins, H., 41
Colquitt-Anderson, D., 6, 23
Colton, A. B., 97
Communication and literacy skills, 33
Communities of practice, 92
Community-based learning and research (CBLR), 15–22; community-based research (CBE) model for, 20–21; direct service-learning model for, 17–18; in practice, 17–21; project-based service-learning model of, 18; service-learning consultation project for, 19–20; university model for, 15–17
Community-based research (CBE), 6
Concrete experience, 81, 85
Confucius, 89
Content reflection, 42–43
Contextualized learning, 41
Conway, Texas, 75
Cooperative education, 5–6, 89; at Northeastern University, 91
Cooperative learning, 33–34
Corporation for National and Community Service, 16, 20
Corradi, G., 40

105

106 EXPERIENTIAL EDUCATION

Cowart, M. R., 63
Cress, C. M., 5, 15
Critical inquiry, 43
Critical reasoning skills, 33
Cruz, N., 5
Cunliffe, A. L., 40
Cutforth, N., 6, 15, 20

Dallimore, E., 6, 15, 18
Daniel, M., 20
Davis, C., 63
Department of Education Title III grant, 82, 83
Devlin, J. W., 74
Dewey, J., 3
Direct service-learning model, 17–18
Discipline-Based Service-Learning, 17. *See also* Direct service-learning model
Doherty, A., 31, 33
Donohue, P., 6, 15, 20
Donovan, T., 1, 89
Dunn, D., 69

Elig, N., 25
Elman, S., 56, 57
Engeström, Y., 4
English for Speakers of Other Languages (ESOL), 17
Episteme, 7, 8
Erickson, G. L., 43
Ethical bypassing, 47; engagement principles and practices for, 51; and Ethical Awareness on Co-op course (Northeastern University), 51–52; foregoing, 48–53; teacher training seminar for, 52–53
Ethics in Psychology seminar (Cohen), 47–48
Ewert, A., 56, 59
Experience and Education (Dewey), 3
Experiential education development, 81; and cycle of metaimplementation, 83; funding for, 63–68; implications for future research in, 86; key activities during stages of metaimplementation in, 83–84; learning goals for, 91–92; quality control in, 92; reflective observation on implementation of, 81–86; role of faculty in, 91; strategies for, 90–94
Experiential learning: approaches and forms for, 3–6; assessing, 55–61; and community-based learning and research (CBLR), 15–22; and cooper-

ative education, 5–6; developmental stages and strategic plan development for, 64; formalized strategic plan and grants for, 67; forms and issues in, 3–11; growing and funding programs in, 63–68; and instituting pedagogical change, 69–74; integrated programs in, 66–67; and internships, 4–5; issues in, 6–10; and learning abroad, 23–28; and mission of higher education, 7–9; novice programs in, 64–66; pedagogy in, 9–10; in performing arts, 31–36; putting, into practice, 81–86; and reflection, 95–99; and reflective ethical engagement, 47–54; and service-learning, 5; strategies for planning programs in, 89–94; three campus case studies in, 69–86; and work-based learning, 39–45
Experiential Learning (Kolb), 3–4
Experiential Learning @ PUC (ExL), 81
Experiential Learning Model (Kolb), 81–86
Experiential pedagogy, 10
Eyler, J., 5, 7, 10

Facebook, 93
Faculty, role of, 91
Farrar-Myers, V. A., 69
Fedorko, J., 4
Fish, S., 7, 9, 41
Fleming, N. P., 75
Flyvbjerg, B., 7, 8
Forrest City, Arkansas, 79
Frankish, C. J., 20
Freire, P., 41
Fulbright Scholarship, 25
Furco, A., 16

Gaines-Hanks, N., 27
Galileo Project, 75. *See also* Odyssey Program (Hendrix College)
Gardinier, L., 6, 23
Gathering information, 85
George, M. A., 20
Germany, 78
Gherardi, S., 40
Gibbs, G., 96
Giles, D. E., Jr., 5, 7, 10
Gilman Scholarship, 25
Goal setting, 85
Goethe, J. W. von, 40
Gold, J., 41
Gonzalez, A. M., 27

from many institutions, though, is the concept of integrating general education with the overall educational curriculum. If this is done, general education courses are no longer something to take quickly so they can be checked off; instead, they become part of the educational development of the student. This integration benefits the student, certainly, but also the larger society—baccalaureate graduates steeped in the liberal arts will become future leaders. Having been prepared with a broad knowledge base, our current students will be able to think more critically and make good use of information to solve problems that have not yet even been identified.
ISBN: 978-04706-26344

TL120   **As the Spirit Moves Us: Embracing Spirituality in the Postsecondary Experience**
Katherine Grace Hendrix, Janice D. Hamlet
During the past decade there has been an increased interest in how members of "first-world" countries cope with growing demands on their time, over-stimulation of the senses, increasing crime rates, and a generally hurried existence. Professors are hardly immune from these forces, and the results cascade onto students, communities, and ultimately, society in general. In contrast to the traditional Western forms of education, which address rational consensus whole eschewing the subjective, a holistic pedagogy suggests that engaging spirituality in one's classroom and profession is necessary for addressing concerns regarding human development and achievement. More specifically, scholars now espouse the value of holistic teaching—teaching that encompasses not only the mind but the soul as well. The contributors in this volume offer diverse vantage points from which to understand the impact of spirituality on well-being, its influence on classroom pedagogy and interpersonal relationships with students and colleagues, and its utility as a coping mechanism. The authors use auto-ethnography to capture the diversity of their perspectives and to display the power of the reflective voice.
ISBN: 978-04705-92632

TL119   **Designing Courses for Significant Learning: Voices of Experience**
L. Dee Fink, Arletta Knight Fink
Higher education today is being called on to deliver a new and more powerful kind of education, one that prepares students to be more engaged citizens, better equipped to solve complex problems at work and better prepared to lead meaningful lives individually. To respond to this call, teachers in colleges and universities need to learn how to design more powerful kinds of learning into their courses. In 2003, Dee Fink published a seminal book, *Creating Significant Learning Experiences*, that offered teachers two major tools for meeting this need: the Taxonomy of Significant Learning and the model of Integrated Course Design. Since that time, educators around the world have found Fink's ideas both visionary and inspiring. This issue of *New Directions for Teaching and Learning* contains multiple stories of how college-level teachers have used these ideas in a variety of teaching situations, with subject matter ranging from the sciences to the humanities. Their conclusion? The ideas in Fink's book truly make a difference. When used properly, they lead to major improvements in the level of student engagement and the quality of student learning!
ISBN: 978-04705-54807

TL118   **Internationalizing the Curriculum in Higher Education**
Carolin Kreber
Internationalization is a looming policy issue in higher education—yet precisely what it can add to the student learning experience and what it means with regard to teaching and learning are far too infrequently discussed or written about. This volume explores different meanings and rationales

underlying the notion of internationalization in higher education. Although internationalization efforts in higher education have become increasingly driven by economic considerations, finance is not an appropriate foundation for all initiatives, particularly those at the level of curriculum, where academic, social/cultural, ethical, political and even environmental rationales feature more strongly. The chapter authors provide a rich conceptual basis from which to appreciate concrete efforts directed at internationalizing curricula, and they describe nine cases of internationalization initiatives at the curricular level. The volume further suggests that consideration of internationalization in higher education must look both within specific programs and across programs. It cannot be separated from fundamental questions about the purposes of higher education and the roles of teachers, students, administrators, and the institution as a whole in fulfilling those purposes.
ISBN: 978-04705-37350

TL117   **Improving the Climate for Undergraduate Teaching and Learning in STEM Fields**
Roger G. Baldwin
The quality of undergraduate education in science, technology, engineering, and mathematics (STEM) fields has been a national concern since the time of Sputnik. In spite of many reports on the state of STEM undergraduate education and multiple reform efforts, time-worn patterns of instruction persist in many STEM classrooms and laboratories. It is increasingly clear that major improvements to STEM under-graduate education require the interest and active engagement of key stakeholders, including STEM instructors, academic administrators, disciplinary societies, and government policy-makers. This volume looks at the challenges of enhancing STEM education from the perspective of these different stakeholders. Each chapter provides an illumi-nating analysis of problems facing STEM education and suggests actions needed to strengthen STEM undergraduate education in a time when science and technology competence are more important than ever. The strategies advanced in this volume should be key elements of the coordinated, systemic effort necessary to implement lasting reform of STEM undergraduate education.
ISBN: 978-04704-97289

TL116   **Team-Based Learning: Small-Group Learning's Next Big Step**
Larry K. Michaelsen, Michael Sweet, Dean X. Parmelee
Team-Based Learning (TBL) is a unique form of small-group learning designed in and for the college classroom. TBL's special combination of incentives and corrective feedback quickly transforms groups into high-performance learning teams, with no time taken from the coverage of course content. In this issue of *New Directions for Teaching and Learning*, the authors describe the practical elements of TBL, how it can look in the classroom, and what they have learned as it has grown into an inter-disciplinary and international practice. Importantly, TBL is not about teaching but about learning. Several articles in this volume illustrate this emphasis by using TBL students' own words to reinforce key ideas.
ISBN: 978-04704-62126

TL115   **The Role of the Classroom in College Student Persistence**
John M. Braxton
This issue of *New Directions for Teaching and Learning* brings into sharp focus the complex role college and university faculty play in shaping the persistence and departure decisions of undergraduate students. The authors review practices ranging from curricular structures and instructional staffing policies to faculty teaching methods, and they offer recommendations for many common problems. Taken together, the chapters outline the elements

of a scholarship of practice centered on keeping students in school. College and university presidents, chief academic affairs officers, academic deans, directors and staff members of campus-based centers for teaching, and individuals responsible for enrollment management will find a great deal of practical wisdom in this volume.
ISBN: 978-04704-22168

TL114   Information Literacy: One Key to Education
Margit Misangyi Watts
This issue draws on the expertise of librarians and faculty to highlight the central role of information literacy in higher education. The authors show how approaches to information literacy can be used to engage undergraduates in research and creative scholarship. The articles clarify definitions of information literacy and illustrate various means of curricular integration. Students regularly miss the relationship between the information-seeking process and the actual creation of knowledge. The authors in this issue support infusing the undergraduate curriculum with research-based learning to facilitate students' ability to define research for themselves. Most importantly, this volume argues, students' information literacy leads beyond finding information—it actually involves their creating knowledge. Education should focus on inquiry, research, and discovery as a frame of mind. Our goal as educators should be to maintain and strengthen the *context* of learning while enhancing the *content* of a liberal education. This finally rests—as it always has—on a foundation of incorporating information literacy skills. Recent dramatic changes in the meaning of "information literacy" have left many educators scrambling to keep up. What has not changed is the importance of teaching students to find information that matters and then helping them figure out *why* it matters. These chapters can help us all integrate the new world of digital information into a relevant, timely approach to content and teaching practice.
ISBN: 978-04703-98715

TL113   Educating Integrated Professionals: Theory and Practice on Preparation for the Professoriate
Carol L. Colbeck, KerryAnn O'Meara, Ann E. Austin
This volume explores how to enhance doctoral education by preparing future faculty to integrate their work in two interrelated ways. The first mode encourages doctoral students—and their faculty mentors—to take advantage of the synergies among their teaching, research, and community service roles. The second mode of integration emphasizes connections between professional and academic aspects of faculty work. The authors draw on theories of identity development, professionalization, apprenticeship, socialization, mentoring, social networks, situated curriculum, concurrent curricula, and academic planning to illuminate some of the drawbacks of current education for the professoriate. They also point toward current programs and new possibilities for educating doctoral students who will be ready to begin their faculty careers as professionals who integrate teaching, research, and service.
ISBN: 978-04702-95403

TL112   Curriculum Development in Higher Education: Faculty-Driven Processes and Practices
Peter Wolf, Julia Christensen Hughes
Faculty within institutions of higher education are increasingly being asked to play leadership roles in curriculum assessment and reform initiatives. This change is being driven by quality concerns; burgeoning disciplinary knowledge; interest in a broader array of learning outcomes, including skills and values; and growing support for constructivist pedagogies and learning-centered, interdisciplinary curricula. It is essential that faculty be well

prepared to take a scholarly approach to this work. To that end, this issue of *New Directions for Teaching and Learning* presents the frameworks used and lessons learned by faculty, administrators, and educational developers in a variety of curriculum assessment and development processes. Collectively, the authors in this volume present the context and catalysts of higher education curriculum reform, advocate for the Scholarship of Curriculum Practice (SoCP), provide examples of curricular assessment and development initiatives at a variety of institutional levels, suggest that educational developers can provide much support to such processes, and argue that this work has profound implications for the faculty role. Anyone involved in curriculum assessment and development will find food for thought in each chapter. ISBN: 978-04702-78512

TL111   Scholarship of Multicultural Teaching and Learning
         Matthew Kaplan, A.T. Miller
         Because effective approaches to multicultural teaching and learning are still being developed in institutions across the U.S. and around the world, it is essential to study and document promising practices. It is only through rigorous research and comparative studies that we can be assured that the significant investments many institutions are making in multicultural education for the development of individual student and faculty skills, and the overall betterment of society, will reap positive results. This volume of *New Directions for Teaching and Learning* provides the valuable results of such research as well as models for the types of research that others could carry out in this area. The volume will appeal to new and experienced practitioners of multicultural teaching. It offers documented illustrations of how such teaching is designed, carried out, and is effective in varied higher education contexts and in a wide range of disciplines representing the humanities, social sciences, engineering and math, and the arts. ISBN: 978-04702-23826

TL110   Neither White Nor Male: Female Faculty of Color
         Katherine Grace Hendrix
         Given limited information on the academic experience in general and on the pedagogical strategies and strengths of faculty of color in particular, the scholars in this issue have come together to begin the process of articulating the academic experiences of female professors of color. While chronicling our challenges within academia as well as our contributions to the education of U.S. students, this collaborative effort will add depth to the existing literature on faculty of color, serve as a reference for positioning women of color within the larger context of higher education (moving us from the margin to the center), and lay a foundation for more inclusive future research. ISBN: 04702-2382-6

TL109   Self-Authorship: Advancing Students' Intellectual Growth
         Peggy S. Meszaros
         This issue addresses the limitations of national efforts to focus students' intellectual development narrowly on testing and explores why educators in higher education should consider using the lens of self-authorship and the Learning Partnerships Model for a more holistic model of student intellectual development. The chapters provide examples of institutional transformations needed to support change in teaching and learning and examples of assessment, research, and curricular development based in self-authorship theory. The summary chapter by Marcia Baxter Magolda ties the themes from each of the chapters together and offers promise for the future. The final chapter provides ideas for next steps in promoting the use of self-authorship to advance the intellectual development of college students. The audience for this volume is broad, ranging from college faculty to student affairs faculty and staff to college administrators who are facing assessment

challenges for reporting student learning outcomes to their various constituencies, agencies, and boards. This volume should also prove instructive to
faculty embarking on curriculum revisions and identifying and measuring
student learning outcomes for undergraduate and graduate students.
ISBN: 07879-9721-2

TL108   **Developing Student Expertise and Community: Lessons from How People Learn**
Anthony J. Petrosino, Taylor Martin, Vanessa Svihla
This issue presents research from a collaboration among learning scientists,
assessment experts, technologists, and subject-matter experts, with the
goal of producing adaptive expertise in students. The model is based on the
National Research Council book *How People Learn.* The chapters present
case studies of working together to develop learning environments centered
on challenge-based instruction. While the strategies and research come from
engineering, they are applicable across disciplines to help students think
about the process of problem solving.
ISBN: 07879-9574-6

TL107   **Exploring Research-Based Teaching**
Carolin Kreber
Investigates the wide scope research-based teaching, while focusing on two
distinct forms. The first sees research-based teaching as student-focused,
inquiry-based learning; students become generators of knowledge. The
second perspective fixes the lens on teachers; the teaching is characterized
by discipline-specific inquiry into the teaching process itself. Both methods
have positive effects on student learning, and this volume explores research
and case studies.
ISBN: 07879-9077-9

TL106   **Supplemental Instruction: New Visions for Empowering Student Learning**
Marion E. Stone, Glen Jacobs
Supplemental Instruction (SI) is an academic support model introduced over
thirty years ago to help students be successful in difficult courses. SI teaches
students how to learn via regularly scheduled, out-of-class collaborative
sessions with other students. This volume both introduces the tenets of SI
to beginners and brings those familiar up to speed with today's methods and
the future directions. Includes case studies, how-to's, benefits to students
and faculty, and more.
ISBN: 0-7879-8680-1

TL105   **A Laboratory for Public Scholarship and Democracy**
Rosa A. Eberly, Jeremy Cohen
Public scholarship has grown out of the scholarship-and-service model, but
its end is democracy rather than volunteerism. The academy has intellectual
and creative resources that can help build involved, democratic communities
through public scholarship. Chapters present concepts, processes, and case
studies from Penn State's experience with public scholarship.
ISBN: 0-7879-8530-9

TL104   **Spirituality in Higher Education**
Sherry L. Hoppe, Bruce W. Speck
With chapters by faculty and administrators, this book investigates the role
of spirituality in educating the whole student while recognizing that how
spirituality is viewed, taught, and experienced is intensely personal. The goal
is not to prescribe a method for integrating spirituality but to offer options
and perspectives. Readers will be reminded that the quest for truth and
meaning, not the destination, is what is vitally important.
ISBN: 0-7879-8363-2

TL103   Identity, Learning, and the Liberal Arts
        Ned Scott Laff
        Argues that we must foster conversations between liberal studies and student
        development theory, because the skills inherent in liberal learning are the
        same skills used for personal development. Students need to experience core
        learning that truly influences their critical thinking skills, character
        development, and ethics. Educators need to design student learning
        encounters that develop these areas. This volume gives examples of how
        liberal arts education can be a healthy foundation for life skills.
        ISBN: 0-7879-8333-0

TL102   Advancing Faculty Learning Through Interdisciplinary Collaboration
        Elizabeth G. Creamer, Lisa R. Lattuca
        Explores why stakeholders in higher education should refocus attention on
        collaboration as a form of faculty learning. Chapters give theoretical basis
        then practical case studies for collaboration's benefits in outreach,
        scholarship, and teaching. Also discusses impacts on education policy,
        faculty hiring and development, and assessment of collaborative work.
        ISBN: 0-7879-8070-6

TL101   Enhancing Learning with Laptops in the Classroom
        Linda B. Nilson, Barbara E. Weaver
        This volume contains case studies—mostly from Clemson University's
        leading-edge laptop program—that address victories as well as glitches in
        teaching with laptop computers in the classroom. Disciplines using laptops
        include psychology, music, statistics, animal sciences, and humanities. The
        volume also advises faculty on making a laptop mandate successful at their
        university, with practical guidance for both pedagogy and student learning.
        ISBN: 0-7879-8049-8

TL100   Alternative Strategies for Evaluating Student Learning
        Michelle V. Achacoso, Marilla D. Svinicki
        Teaching methods are adapting to the modern era, but innovation in
        assessment of student learning lags behind. This volume examines
        theory and practical examples of creative new methods of evaluation,
        including authentic testing, testing with multimedia, portfolios, group
        exams, visual synthesis, and performance-based testing. Also investigates
        improving students' ability to take and learn from tests, before and after.
        ISBN: 0-7879-7970-8

TL99   Addressing Faculty and Student Classroom Improprieties
        John M. Braxton, Alan E. Bayer
        Covers the results of a large research study on occurrence and perceptions
        of classroom improprieties by both students and faculty. When classroom
        norms are violated, all parties in a classroom are affected, and teaching and
        learning suffer. The authors offer guidelines for both student and faculty
        classroom behavior and how institutions might implement those suggestions.
        ISBN: 0-7879-7794-2

TL98   Decoding the Disciplines: Helping Students Learn Disciplinary Ways of
        Thinking
        David Pace, Joan Middendorf
        The Decoding the Disciplines model is a way to teach students the critical-
        thinking skills required to understand their specific discipline. Faculty define
        bottlenecks to learning, dissect the ways experts deal with the problematic
        issues, and invent ways to model experts' thinking for students. Chapters are
        written by faculty in diverse fields who successfully used these methods and
        became involved in the scholarship of teaching and learning.
        ISBN: 0-7879-7789-6

TL97   **Building Faculty Learning Communities**
Milton D. Cox, Laurie Richlin
A very effective way to address institutional challenges is a faculty learning community. FLCs are useful for preparing future faculty, reinvigorating senior faculty, and implementing new courses, curricula, or campus initiatives. The results of FLCs parallel those of student learning communities, such as retention, deeper learning, respect for others, and greater civic participation. This volume describes FLCs from a practitioner's perspective, with plenty of advice, wisdom, and lessons for starting your own FLC.
ISBN: 0-7879-7568-0

TL96   **Online Student Ratings of Instruction**
Trav D. Johnson, D. Lynn Sorenson
Many institutions are adopting Web-based student ratings of instruction, or are considering doing it, because online systems have the potential to save time and money among other benefits. But they also present a number of challenges. The authors of this volume have firsthand experience with electronic ratings of instruction. They identify the advantages, consider costs and benefits, explain their solutions, and provide recommendations on how to facilitate online ratings.
ISBN: 0-7879-7262-2

TL95   **Problem-Based Learning in the Information Age**
Dave S. Knowlton, David C. Sharp
Provides information about theories and practices associated with problem-based learning, a pedagogy that allows students to become more engaged in their own education by actively interpreting information. Today's professors are adopting problem-based learning across all disciplines to faciliate a broader, modern definition of what it means to learn. Authors provide practical experience about designing useful problems, creating conducive learning environments, facilitating students' activities, and assessing students' efforts at problem solving.
ISBN: 0-7879-7172-3

TL94   **Technology: Taking the Distance out of Learning**
Margit Misangyi Watts
This volume addresses the possibilities and challenges of computer technology in higher education. The contributors examine the pressures to use technology, the reasons not to, the benefits of it, the feeling of being a learner as well as a teacher, the role of distance education, and the place of computers in the modern world. Rather than discussing only specific successes or failures, this issue addresses computers as a new cultural symbol and begins meaningful conversations about technology in general and how it affects education in particular.
ISBN: 0-7879-6989-3

TL93   **Valuing and Supporting Undergraduate Research**
Joyce Kinkead
The authors gathered in this volume share a deep belief in the value of undergraduate research. Research helps students develop skills in problem solving, critical thinking, and communication, and undergraduate researchers' work can contribute to an institution's quest to further knowledge and help meet societal challenges. Chapters provide an overview of undergraduate research, explore programs at different types of institutions, and offer suggestions on how faculty members can find ways to work with undergraduate researchers.
ISBN: 0-7879-6907-9

NEW DIRECTIONS FOR TEACHING AND LEARNING

ORDER FORM SUBSCRIPTION AND SINGLE ISSUES

DISCOUNTED BACK ISSUES:

Use this form to receive 20% off all back issues of *New Directions for Teaching and Learning*.
All single issues priced at **$23.20** (normally $29.00)

TITLE	ISSUE NO.	ISBN
_____	_____	_____
_____	_____	_____
_____	_____	_____

Call 888-378-2537 or see mailing instructions below. When calling, mention the promotional code JBNND to receive your discount. For a complete list of issues, please visit www.josseybass.com/go/ndtl

SUBSCRIPTIONS: (1 YEAR, 4 ISSUES)

☐ New Order   ☐ Renewal

U.S.	☐ Individual: $89	☐ Institutional: $259
CANADA/MEXICO	☐ Individual: $89	☐ Institutional: $299
ALL OTHERS	☐ Individual: $113	☐ Institutional: $333

Call 888-378-2537 or see mailing and pricing instructions below.
Online subscriptions are available at www.onlinelibrary.wiley.com

ORDER TOTALS:

Issue / Subscription Amount: $ _____

Shipping Amount: $ _____
(for single issues only – subscription prices include shipping)

Total Amount: $ _____

SHIPPING CHARGES:

First Item $5.00
Each Add'l Item $3.00

(No sales tax for U.S. subscriptions. Canadian residents, add GST for subscription orders. Individual rate subscriptions must be paid by personal check or credit card. Individual rate subscriptions may not be resold as library copies.)

BILLING & SHIPPING INFORMATION:

☐ **PAYMENT ENCLOSED:** *(U.S. check or money order only. All payments must be in U.S. dollars.)*

☐ **CREDIT CARD:** ☐VISA ☐MC ☐AMEX

Card number _____Exp. Date_____

Card Holder Name_____Card Issue # _____

Signature _____Day Phone _____

☐ **BILL ME:** *(U.S. institutional orders only. Purchase order required.)*

Purchase order # _____
Federal Tax ID 13559302 • GST 89102-8052

Name_____

Address_____

Phone_____ E-mail_____

Copy or detach page and send to: **John Wiley & Sons, PTSC, 5th Floor**
989 Market Street, San Francisco, CA 94103-1741

Order Form can also be faxed to: **888-481-2665**

PROMO JBNND

Statement of Ownership

Statement of Ownership, Management, and Circulation (required by 39 U.S.C. 3685), filed on OCTOBER 1,2010 for NEW DIRECTIONS FOR TEACHING AND LEARNING (Publication No. 0271-0633), published Quarterly at Wiley Subscription Services, Inc., at Jossey-Bass, 989 Market St., San Francisco, CA 94103..

The names and complete mailing addresses of the Publisher, Editor, and Managing Editor are: Publisher, Wiley Subscription Services Inc., A Wiley Company at San Francisco, 989 Market St., San Francisco, CA 94103-1741; Editor, Catherine M. Wehlburg, TCU Box 297098, Texas Christian University, Fort Worth TX 76129; Managing Editor, None,.

NEW DIRECTIONS FOR TEACHING AND LEARNING is a publication owned by Wiley Subscription Services, Inc.. The known bondholders, mortgagees, and other security holders owning or holding 1% or more of total amount of bonds, mortgages, or other securities are (see list).

	Average No. Copies Each Issue During Preceding 12 Months	No. Copies Of Single Issue Published Nearest To Filing Date (Summer 2010)
15a. Total number of copies (net press run)	1,090	1,047
15b. Legitimate paid and/or requested distribution (by mail and outside mail)		
15b(1). Individual paid/requested mail subscriptions stated on PS form 3541 (include direct written request from recipient, telemarketing, and Internet requests from recipient, paid subscriptions including nominal rate subscriptions, advertiser's proof copies, and exchange copies)	480	438
15b(2). Copies requested by employers for distribution to employees by name or position, stated on PS form 3541	0	0
15b(3). Sales through dealers and carriers, street vendors, counter sales, and other paid or requested distribution outside USPS	0	0
15b(4). Requested copies distributed by other mail classes through USPS	0	0
15c. Total paid and/or requested circulation (sum of 15b(1), (2), (3), and (4))	480	438
15d. Nonrequested distribution (by mail and outside mail)		
15d(1). Outside county nonrequested copies stated on PS form 3541	9	13
15d(2). In-county nonrequested copies stated on PS form 3541	0	0
15d(3). Nonrequested copies distributed through the USPS by other classes of mail	0	0
15d(4). Nonrequested copies distributed outside the mail	0	0
15e. Total nonrequested distribution (sum of 15d(1), (2), (3), and (4))	9	13
15f. Total distribution (sum of 15c and 15e)	489	451
15g. Copies not distributed	601	596
15h. Total (sum of 15f and 15g)	1,090	1,047
15i. Percent paid and/or requested circulation (15c divided by 15f times 100)	98.1%	97.1%

I certify that all information furnished on this form is true and complete. I understand that anyone who furnishes false or misleading information on this form or who omits material or information requested on this form may be subject to criminal sanctions (including fines and imprisonment) and/or civil sanctions (including civil penalties).

(signed) Susan E. Lewis, VP & Publisher-Periodicals